A HISTORY OF YORKSHIRE CRICKET

Other Cricket Books by J. M. Kilburn

IN SEARCH OF CRICKET

THE SCARBOROUGH CRICKET FESTIVAL

YORKSHIRE: COUNTY CRICKET SERIES

LEN HUTTON: A PORTRAIT

HISTORY OF YORKSHIRE C.C.C. 1924–1949

HOMES OF SPORT: CRICKET (WITH N. W. D. YARDLEY)

CRICKET DECADE

A HISTORY OF YORKSHIRE CRICKET

J. M. Kilburn

STANLEY PAUL/LONDON

STANLEY PAUL & CO LTD
178–202 Great Portland Street, London W1
AN IMPRINT OF THE HUTCHINSON GROUP
London Melbourne Sydney Auckland
Bombay Toronto Johannesburg New York

First published 1970

This book has been set in Baskerville, printed in Great Britain on Antique Wove paper by Anchor Press, and bound by Wm. Brendon, both of Tiptree, Essex
ISBN 0 09 101110 8

CONTENTS

ILLUSTRATIONS

I

Local habitation and a name

Yorkshire played as a self-styled county team long before the formation of the official club in 1863 and cricket in Yorkshire had attained distinction in centres as widely separated within the county as Sheffield in the south and Bedale in the north early in the 19th century. There was, however, no county co-ordination and little call for it until the counties began to create their own importance as the famous touring teams of All England and United England disintegrated.

Sheffield took the lead in forming a Yorkshire County Cricket Club because the appropriate facilities were available there. Sheffield wanted representative cricket as public attraction to the Bramall Lane sports ground opened in 1855; Sheffield enjoyed the tradition of matches with Nottingham which had been 'county' occasions for nearly 100 years; Sheffield had a powerful patron, and player, of cricket in M. J. Ellison, agent to the Duke of Norfolk who was Sheffield's principal landlord. Sheffield had also a convenient place of assembly in the Adelphi hotel, kept by Harry Sampson, who was a local cricketing celebrity as a member of the United England Eleven and conqueror of Tom Marsden in a single-wicket money match of 1841.

Sampson was a tiny fellow, five feet four inches in height, but his batting was impressive in its 'fine back play' and his hardihood was not to be questioned. He fielded long stop, which was a perilous occupation on the rough outfields of his day, and he is credited with the record individual score on ice, earned by an innings of 162 played in February 1841.

Harry Sampson was 'host' to the inaugural meeting of the Yorkshire County Cricket Club but M. J. Ellison was the moving spirit of the new organisation. He was also to a considerable extent its financial stability. Much of the club's early expenditure was met from his own pocket and the books kept by M. J. Ellison as Treasurer never revealed details of the generosity extended by the same M. J. Ellison as President.

The young Yorkshire club and most other first-class cricket of the time in its county form subsisted on private patronage. Players were paid to play but administrators frequently paid to serve and moneyed enthusiasts were ready sponsors for teams or matches.

Yorkshire's early professionals were freelance cricketers and made a thin living from the game. The usual match fee was £5, from which travelling and living expenses had to be paid, and there were times when players returned from an engagement with empty pockets and no contribution towards household obligations.

A suspicion that William Clarke, as promoter and manager, was maintaining an unreasonable financial advantage over the players initiated the disintegration of the All England Eleven, but when the new Yorkshire club came into dispute with leading players the point at issue was one of principle more than of pay.

In 1865 Yorkshire arranged fixtures with Surrey, Kent and the South of England, but the Yorkshire captain, George Anderson, declined office and four of the most prominent players, G. Atkinson, R. Iddison, J. Rowbotham and E. Stephenson, refused to play against Surrey. Their decision followed a disagreement that had arisen three years earlier during a match between the All England Eleven and Surrey at the Oval when Surrey were accused of appointing an umpire specifically to no-ball Edgar Willsher, one of the All England bowlers. In consequence southern players formed a United South team in rivalry to the All England Eleven, and George Anderson, who had long been a regular and respected member of All England, announced that he 'would not play against those who have combined to sweep us from the cricket field altogether if they could'.

George Anderson's influence, on the field and off, was powerful. He was greatly admired as a player and as a man. He came from the north Yorkshire market town of Bedale, which was an important cricketing centre in the county, and he was persuaded into the All England Eleven in 1851 after William Clarke had made a coaching visit to Bedale.

With Clarke's successor, George Parr, Anderson toured Australia and New Zealand in 1863-4 and in his twenty years with the All England Eleven he travelled almost everywhere in the British Isles. His cricketing strength lay in his batting, which was by nature forceful and was particularly valuable when conditions or circumstances were most difficult.

All his contemporaries spoke well of him. William Caffyn, who played with Anderson in the All England Eleven and toured with him in Australia and New Zealand, expressed wholehearted admiration for Anderson's ability to 'come off when others were unable to score'. Looking back over 40 years Caffyn focussed a personal picture of his old cricketing companion, seeing a 'fine strapping fellow, six feet high in his stockings. He had quite a military appearance when in ordinary dress and he nearly always wore a suit of heather mixture.'

A suit of heather mixture was not Anderson's playing attire, of course. For cricket he changed to the costume of his time, which was represented by a coloured shirt, usually striped or spotted, with a collar and tie; trousers were white or approximately so, supported by a heavy belt with a big metal buckle after the wide braces of the late 18th century had passed out of fashion. Boots were brown. Beards, full or as a fringe, were commonplace. Anderson was dark-haired and bearded and is shown serious of countenance in contempoary pictures, though posing for pictures could in itself have been counted a serious undertaking.

George Anderson was certainly not of gloomy disposition. He enjoyed his sporting activities. He took part in the athletics competitions and exhibitions that frequently followed an early finish to a cricket match. He enjoyed a day's shooting and rated his own experience 'a happy and healthful life'.

Anderson's difference with Yorkshire in 1865 was in no sense a quarrel with the county authority. He declined the offer of the Yorkshire captaincy with respectful dignity on a principle of loyalty to earlier playing colleagues and he kept the goodwill of Yorkshire players and officials, commending young cricketers to their attention to the end of his days.

His companions in revolt returned to the Yorkshire fold in 1867 and all the seven matches arranged by the county committee were won. Iddison and Stephenson made useful batting contributions to these victories but the factor of determination was clearly the bowling of George Freeman, who took 51 wickets in six matches. Twice in the season, against Surrey and against Lancashire, he and Luke Greenwood bowled unchanged through both innings.

George Freeman won and earned a tremendous reputation in a short career. He appears in the Yorkshire records as having played from 1865 to 1881, but in his first two seasons and his last three he took part in only one county game and it was in the five years between 1867 and 1871 that he made his enduring name in cricket.

Freeman was a fast bowler, born and brought up in Boroughbridge, with Malton claiming him through association as a professional player and Thirsk adopting him by later residential qualification when he entered business as an auctioneer. He was a fast bowler of the quality to draw highest praise from W. G. Grace, who was inclined to be scornful of fast bowling as a matter of principle and practice. Freeman returned compliment for compliment. Of an innings by Grace played against Yorkshire at Lord's in 1870 Freeman declared: 'A more wonderful innings was never played. It was a marvel the doctor was not either maimed or unnerved for the rest of his days, or killed outright.' As the ball was 'flying about ribs, shoulders and head' the Lord's pitch of the period seems to have left some room for improvement.

Freeman was not terrifying through an intimidating approach to the bowling crease or through any exhibition of ill-nature. He was jovial in disposition, completely trustworthy in public business and affectionate in private friendship. In later life he became full bearded but portraits from playing days show him with moustache and sidewhiskers on a round, placid face. He was sturdily built, though not of great height, and his physical strength, with the athlete's co-ordination, gave him the basis for bowling resources. His run-up was short, with a long delivery stride, and though his arm would be considered intolerably low by modern standards in his own time it was remarked on as 'suspiciously' high, for the change from below the shoulder delivery was being accepted only with reluctance among older cricketers.

Contemporary observation attributed Freeman's devastating break-back to a 'twist of the elbow'. By 'twist' or by finger-cut Freeman certainly brought the ball back from the off to disconcerting effect. He is credited with an ability to bowl shooters and no doubt the round-arm action of his time would accentuate this tendency, but variation in lift must have been essentially the product of ill-prepared pitches. Batting was always a hazardous undertaking before the era of the heavy roller and carefully tended turf. Against bowlers of the Freeman manner and accomplishment it was invariably either a brief or a painful undertaking and the conquest of fast bowling by W. G. Grace was at a cost of the thighs reduced to a mass of bruises.

Professional cricketers of Freeman's time could not have made a living from the county clubs whose fixture lists were short, but income came through local engagements and appearances for representative sides in all parts of the country. Before 1873, when qualification rules were introduced, players could and did appear for more than one county in the same season.

Roger Iddison, an all-rounder from Bedale, was Yorkshire's nominated captain from 1863 to 1870, but he played for both Yorkshire and Lancashire, recording Lancashire's first county century, against Surrey, in 1866 and altogether representing Lancashire 16 times before the rules confined him to his first choice of Yorkshire. County matches were frequently so styled without being the direct promotion of the official county clubs and the peripatetic professional willing to undertake awkward journeys could usually find a match fee and scope for talent money somewhere in England from May to September.

For the busy cricketer travelling was arduous and living away from home inclined to be rough. Sometimes the match fees covered expenses, sometimes the pocket was empty on the homeward journey. The ale-house was an attraction, the sycophant a tempter, but professional cricket provided a freemasonry that opened doors from the grim life of factory and mine and the bondage of agricultural labour. Cricketers knew each other and helped each other.

In August 1869 Yorkshire were in London on a Saturday evening with an engagement against Surrey due to begin on Monday. Freeman and Luke Greenwood had been injured in a road accident and had no hope of being able to play and in the players' discussion on replacements the name of Ephriam Lockwood was put forward.

Lockwood was sent for because his uncle, John Thewlis, was in the Yorkshire side and because Thewlis and Greenwood had in their own achievements established the merits and potentialities of cricketers from the community of Lascelles Hall. The 23-year-old Lockwood arrived in London on his first visit with a bat in his hand and his playing trousers and shirt in a paper parcel under his arm. He was welcomed to his first county experience with characteristic Yorkshire encouragement cloaked in foreboding. Uncle John Thewlis told him that unless he proved worthy of selection he would never return to Lascelles Hall alive. During his innings Lockwood was sternly warned: 'Remember, tha's on thi merits.'

On the field Lockwood drew first attention to himself through trousers that had shrunk in much washing and a shirt of red, green and black squares. The Oval spectators chaffed him as Yorkshire fielded through a Surrey innings of 195 and chaffed him further when he opened the Yorkshire batting with Thewlis. To their credit the crowd turned their good-natured banter to wholehearted admiration as the unknown from provincial darkness revealed his ability. Thewlis and Lockwood, uncle and nephew from Lascelles Hall, raised a partnership of 176, and Lockwood in his first innings for Yorkshire, played against unfamiliar bowling in an unfamiliar world, scored 91.

Lockwood continued to play for Yorkshire over a period of 20 years, scoring nearly 8,000 runs and making eight centuries in a period when the individual century was an achievement of remark. He was, of course, involved in much more than Yorkshire cricket, for it was not until the 1880s that counties undertook as many as 20 fixtures in a season. He was among first choices for Players *v.* Gentlemen, North *v.* South and any-representative side collected to meet touring teams. He declined, for one reason or another, several invitations to play in Australia, but he went to America with Richard Daft's team in 1879 and by all accounts enjoyed everything except mosquitoes.

The outstanding feature of Lockwood's batting was off-side play. He was not powerfully built, but early training on the roadway with improvised bat and ball from the weaving shed gave him a quick eye and sharp reactions and he became renowned for his square-cutting which at times almost miraculously took the ball from the stumps. His highest county innings was played late in his career when he made 208 for Yorkshire against Kent at Gravesend, but the Oval, where he began so well, seemed his regular inspiration. There he made two of his Yorkshire centuries and scores of 91, 96 and 97 and there he became, after his first embarrassing experience, as great a favourite with the crowd as any player of his time.

In 1876 Lockwood became Yorkshire's appointed leader but he was not a successful captain of a successful side. Yorkshire teams of the period contained exceptional individual talent but they had no unifying force, no fusion of identity.

They played day by day, match by match, under the inspiration of the moment rather than with the end product of a championship constantly in mind. They won some notable victories, but they also suffered some humbling defeats.

Accusation has been laid that the day's achievements too frequently reflected indulgences of the night before and that even on the field the cricketers lacked discipline. Little evidence supports the charge. Some cricketers did drink, some no doubt to excess, but a greater number maintained either abstinence or marked moderation. Some cricketers were inclined to earn their match money at the least inconvenience to themselves, but outstanding performances invariably reaped immediate reward in the form of collection, gift or bonus and professionals were in no position to ignore cash considerations.

In the early period of a championship then without official recognition the county clubs were not the significant organisations of later development. They commanded a loyalty from players, but only one loyalty of many. Players carried responsibility to several cricketing units and a primary responsibility to their own livelihood. It is more than coincidence that Gloucestershire and Nottinghamshire were the most successful counties through the 1870s and the 1880s. Gloucestershire had the Graces as the nucleus, Nottinghamshire had a club with elements of exclusiveness based on Trent Bridge. No other county—and only nine or ten counties claimed to be first-class before 1894—had comparable factors of cohesion. The Graces were Gloucestershire and Nottingham was Nottinghamshire.

Yorkshire's players were tremendous in themselves but less than their sum in their occasional association. Decade by decade some player joined the side to become a giant of cricket, but the giants never linked arms nor accepted an overriding directive. The county committee, still virtually a Sheffield representation, could not rule them and they could not rule themselves through the authority of one of their own number elected captain.

The difficulties of captaincy by professional were evident. It is almost impossible for a professional to rule professionals without fear or favour because he has his own professional interests to consider. Endeavours to be placatory to all may lead to weakness, as Lockwood found when his bowlers declined the challenge of unhelpful conditions or batsmen enjoying mastery. A bowling captain may, through misplaced modesty, bowl himself too sparingly as Emmett probably did.

Tom Emmett, born in Halifax, could scarcely have bowled himself too much by contemporary opinion. He was ranked among the highest by the highest. W. G. Grace said of him that on his day he was unplayable and confessed that more than once, when well set, he had been bowled by Emmett with a ball that would always beat him or anyone.

The ball was the bowler's dream, pitching on or outside the leg stump and hitting the top of the off. Emmett bowled it at a lively pace and it brought him world-wide renown.

He was a left-hander who came into Yorkshire cricket, for one match, in 1866 on the strength of his performances in the Keighley district where he had been professional to the Keighley club and augmented his income by appearances for district teams raised to challenge the touring All-England Elevens. In 1867 Emmett came to his first Yorkshire bowling triumph, taking six wickets for seven runs against Surrey and thereafter for 20 years he remained a leading figure of the cricket fields.

For Yorkshire alone Emmett is credited with 1,269 wickets, bowling in 299 matches, and, of course, he took many more wickets playing for representative sides at first-class level. He went to Australia three times and to America with Richard Daft's team and everywhere he was as successful a player as he was a welcome travelling companion. Tom Emmett rejoiced in cricket and the cricketer's life.

He became known as both a magnificent player and as a 'character'. He was popular because of his enthusiasm for play; he was memorable because of his sharp wit, uninhibited comment and unfailing readiness to make good-humoured capital from his own discomfiture.

In sufferings at sea he was prepared to joke on the need for a heavy roller on the 'pitch'. Yorkshire were playing M.C.C. at Lord's the day after W. G. Grace had completed medical qualifications and become proud possessor of his diploma. Emmett, fielding cover point, slipped and fell on muddy ground in stopping a hard off-drive. 'Are you hurt?' Grace asked the fallen fieldsman. 'No,' replied Emmett, ruefully surveying the dark stain on his trousers. 'I've got my diploma.'

Grace and Emmett had the respect of great players for each other's talents and on the occasion of an innings of 300 by Grace Emmett summarised the day's play in a phrase that has become a classic of cricket. 'Grace before meat,' he said. 'Grace after meat. Grace all the bloomin' day.'

Witticisms gained added flavour from their 'deadpan' delivery. Emmett had a long, rather lugubrious face with a nose that attracted remark for both its size and colour, but Emmett's career was too long and his form too consistent for the inevitable allusions to have any serious justification. Emmett played in Yorkshire teams from 1866 to 1888 and was the county's appointed captain for five seasons.

He was not a successful captain by measure of results. Through his years of office, from 1878 to 1882, Yorkshire were never rated champion county in the end-of-season assessment that had no official standing and in most of the seasons they were as liable to suffer a humiliating defeat as they were to achieve a notable victory.

They were an unreliable side, probably because they were an assembly of individuals without any incentive to mould themselves into a unit. They lost, they won, they departed their various ways until called on for another match. Players were offered no continuity of engagement and the county club had no assurance of players' availability. Yorkshire had great cricketers and the making of a great team but before the early 1880s nobody undertook the responsibility for creating dedication and welfare.

2

Picking up wrinkles

Martin Bladen Hawke was introduced into Yorkshire county cricket by favouritism. He was invited to play in the Scarborough Festival, or Carnival, as it was then known, by the Reverend E. S. Carter, who arranged Festival teams. Canon Carter was also a moving spirit in the Yorkshire Gentlemen C.C., based on York, and there he had noted Hawke's enthusiasm, ability and, perhaps most significantly, his availability. The Hon. M. B. Hawke was awarded a cricket 'Blue' at Cambridge in 1882 and joined Yorkshire when the university term ended. He was invited, no doubt in accordance with the social decencies, to act as captain, but he declined, saying to Emmett: 'I prefer to play under you and pick up a few wrinkles.'

He picked up a 'few wrinkles' and a life-long interest. Martin Bladen, seventh Baron Hawke from 1888, was captain of Yorkshire for 27 seasons and President of the county club for 40 years.

When he came into his cricketing inheritance he found an abundance of ability but little sign of cohesion and direction. The talent on view included Emmett's fast-medium left-arm bowling, Peate's slow left-arm bowling, fast right-arm bowling by G. P. Harrison, batting of varied character by Louis Hall, Lockwood, Ulyett and Bates with Joseph Hunter as successor in wicketkeeping to the heroic Pinder whose hands were damaged to distortion through taking fast bowling on rough pitches for nearly 20 years.

The new captain's impact was not immediately evident, Yorkshire through the 1880s continued to be an unreliable side, mingling brilliant achievement with miserable performance. In a decade they won far less than half their matches and in their most disappointing seasons they became known as a fielding side so fallible that 'they were too polite to run anyone out'.

Disappointment began to express itself in complaint against the county club management which was virtually a Sheffield monopoly, although in 1883 committee representation was conceded to seven other districts and county matches and team selections were never concentrated on Sheffield interests.

Hawke's early years of captaincy were spent in apprenticeship to the trade of captaincy. The 'Hon. gentleman's captaincy was highly commended' in the committee minute book, but inevitably it was captaincy in name and by the formalities more than leadership through authority of performance. The Honourable undergraduate was among his seniors in age and experience and his peers in cricketing ability.

Two significant qualities quickly became evident. Hawke enjoyed the cricketer's life—from the comparative comfort of the amateur ranks—and he appreciated the virtues of his players. The first generation of Yorkshire cricketers under his command never came as close to his heart as those he moulded to the pattern of his choice, but they were given his sympathy and his praise. He treasured the drolleries of Tom Emmett. He wrote of George Ulyett as 'a grand Yorkshireman, big and big-hearted, burly and a powerful smiter'. He thought Edmund Peate 'a really charming fellow . . . blessed with the most perfect action'. He rated William Bates 'the most engaging of all professional run-getters'.

From these players he learned much of cricket's technicalities on the field. Through these players he came to understand professional problems and discover the ways to realisation of his own expanding ambition in cricket.

The 'grand Yorkshireman', George Ulyett, was born in Sheffield and with the exceptional physique evident in his boyhood was a natural recruit to the steelworkers. His employment in the rolling mills was sporadic. Cricket matches would keep occupying his attention and his employer's time.

Ulyett followed his bent. He joined the Bradford club as a professional in 1871 and two years later he was playing for Yorkshire. He was included primarily as a bowler, a fast bowler supporting Allan Hill, but he was talented as batsman and fielder and he was enthusiastic in every feature of cricket. As his batting developed he bowled less, but he was a valuable all-rounder at every level to the end of his long career.

It was a career in keeping with character, full of adventure, abounding in achievement and zest. He appeared for Yorkshire in twenty seasons, he went to Australia five times, to South Africa once and to America once. He wrote cricket history all over England and all over the world and when he was not on the field he tumbled into excitement with the inevitability of a wasp tumbling into a jam jar. He was nicknamed 'Happy Jack'.

He played cricket in the only way he knew. He sought always the joy of the moment, the ring of challenge, the fun of the business. With six runs need for a Yorkshire victory and one wicket standing Ulyett was caught on the edge of the boundary driving Johnny Briggs. He saw no need for apology.

Instructed by his captain to 'play steady' at a critical period in a match at Sydney, Ulyett replied, 'But I feel rather like hitting them,' and scored 55 in half an hour.

Bowling to the most powerful hitter of the day in a Test match at Lord's Ulyett caught and bowled G. J. Bonnor in an astonishing feat of achievement and courage. The ball was a straight half-volley and Bonnor drove it from the middle of the bat with all his strength. Ulyett put up his right hand and in the twinkling of an eye the catch was made. 'The ball was no sooner out of my hand than it was back again,' was Ulyett's own summary of the proceedings.

W. G. Grace and Lord Harris, both fielding for England at the time, considered Ulyett foolish for attempting the catch. Had the ball struck his wrist or arm or one finger the outcome would inevitably have been broken bones.

Ulyett never spent much time in consideration of possible consequences. He fell overboard in shark-infested waters during an Australian tour. In New Zealand he had to swim for his life when the coach carrying the players was trapped in the torrent of a flooded gorge. On one visit to London Ulyett and Peate were taking an evening walk down Whitehall when they were attracted by the guests assembling in Downing Street for some formal reception. 'Follow me,' said 'Happy Jack, 'I'm deaf.' Without a ticket, without the formal dress for the occasion—which was in the name of the Prime Minister—Ulyett made his way into the reception room, simply ignoring the queries of attendants. Among invited guests was a noted amateur cricketer to whom Ulyett calmly explained that he had thought he was 'looking in at a place of entertainment'.

Anywhere was a place of entertainment to George Ulyett, even a cricket field during a riot. Enraged spectators breaking the bounds at Sydney when Lord Harris's team were in the field found Ulyett with a stump in each hand and prepared happily for battle. One spectator struck Lord Harris and Ulyett begged permission to 'have a go at him', but while Lord Harris was restraining the eager Ulyett another England player, A. N. Hornby, took the offending spectator by the coat collar, bustled him through the milling crowd to the pavilion and delivered him into police hands.

As a batsman Ulyett was fearless and forceful, as would be expected from his appearance and disposition. His style was not ideal for opening an innings by modern practice, but his figures justified his principles. He made his 1,000 Yorkshire runs in five seasons and his county career aggregate was 16,063. The records give him a share in 14 century partnerships for the first wicket and of these 12 were made with Louis Hall.

Only cricket could have brought into successful partnership such contrasts of character and performance as Ulyett and Hall. Ulyett was a merchant adventurer in the game, prepared to risk his wicket with almost every stroke he made. Hall favoured slow accumulation of capital in gilt-edged security.

Hall first played for Yorkshire in 1873 but he was given little chance to establish himself in the side for several years. He waited patiently.

He was good at waiting and expressed his patience in batting that became legendary for its persistence. At the wicket he stayed and stayed, to the exasperation of opponents and spectators but invariably to the benefit of his own side. In a long innings he welcomed opportunity to complete a century. In shorter innings he 'carried his bat'. In the Yorkshire records there are 17 instances by L Hall of carrying the bat through a completed innings

Contemporaries gave 12 runs an hour as a fair average for his scoring rate but they paid tribute to the skill of his defence and the calmness of his approach to critical situations. Hall carried sobriety at the crease to principles of living and was distinguished among the cricketers of his time in maintaining strict teetotalism. In this insistence he lost no respect and the jokes founded on his excessive leanness of figure were always good-humoured. When a frustrated bowler wished 'someone would stick a pin into Hall', Emmett insisted, 'It wouldn't stick. There isn't enough flesh for a pin to find a cushion.'

Distinction in the cricketing career of Edmund Peate (called Ted) was not in any physical characteristics or qualities of temperament. He was simply a beautiful and effective bowler.

Peate joined Yorkshire in 1879 when he was professional to the Manningham club in Bradford and he played for the county until 1887. His 820 county wickets in 160 matches represented an average of five wickets a match which is high productivity for any type of bowling in any period of cricket. Peate was a fast left-arm bowler in his early club professional engagements but he found his true talent at reduced pace through winter experiment in the shed of a textile mill at which he was employed.

The virtue of his bowling was accuracy and subtle variation of flight rather than any exceptional power of spin. He was the first of the astonishing succession of slow or slow-medium left-handers that extended through Yorkshire cricket for 60 years —Peate, Peel, Rhodes, Verity.

Peate's outstanding performance by figures was his capture of eight Surrey wickets for five runs at Holbeck in 1883, but this was on a soft pitch and a greater technical triumph was represented by his achievement against the touring Australians at Old Trafford in 1884. On a true, hard pitch Peate bowled through both Australian innings. He took five for 28 in 41 overs and five for 23 in 38 overs.

Neither Peate nor Emmett, nor both together over nine

seasons, could bring Yorkshire to leadership among the counties. They remained a side of unco-ordinated talent, a match for the best but a consolation to the worst in vagaries of form. They were an unreliable fielding side and they were without the concentration of county interest that led them to later predominance.

3

Growth of authority

Lord Hawke, in his captaincy, changed the character of Yorkshire cricket. He was never to be ranked among the greatest of players but he was not a handicap to efficiency. He scored over 13,000 runs. Through long experience he came to appreciate the techniques of cricket and the capacities of cricketers. He enjoyed cricket as a pastime and he enjoyed his own influence on cricket as it extended. He accepted authority and the responsibilities of authority. Assuming the privileges of leadership he exercised them with determination to lead.

Lord Hawke's authority in the councils of Yorkshire grew because of the committee reorganisation of 1893 and grew again through his election to the office of President in 1898. For twelve years, until he retired from playing, he was both captain in the field and commander in the committee-room.

In the process of building his own position through the 1890s Lord Hawke was also the architect of Yorkshire eminence. He was gathering round himself cricketers of skill and spirit and he was creating in professional cricket, challenged and flavoured by the amateur element, a pride and satisfaction. Long before Lord Hawke the leading cricketers had been glamorous figures in sport. Lord Hawke helped to add to the glitter of renown a substance of financial stability.

At Lord Hawke's insistence Yorkshire cricketers were given establishment in the society of sport. They ceased to be the hired hands; they became associates. Regularised systems for winter pay, bonus money and benefits were introduced.

Lord Hawke no doubt acted as though Yorkshire cricket were his estate, to be maintained and developed to his liking, but he supervised the estate with untiring enthusiasm and unceasing care for the betterment of its dependants.

At the turn of the century Yorkshire's captain and president came to fulfilment of cricketing ambitions and Yorkshire cricket acquired a reputation and a record that have been treasured heritage ever since. The three seasons of 1900, 1901 and 1902 were a logical culmination to 10 years of cultivation.

The 1890s and the first decade of the 20th century represented cricket's peak as a national game of social acceptability. Cricket then embraced an enviable profession and an amateur pastime, a concern for the proletariat acknowledged by princes. It was a topic for discussion in public house and palace, an approved occupation for lord and labourer. It provided a living and a justification for existence. It was an institution, like the Royal Navy, the golden sovereign or the British empire.

Most of the traditions and customs of first-class cricket were established or consolidated in this period. The first-class counties doubled in number, the county championship was given an official status, a Board of Control for national cricket was created. The shape of the season, with its Test matches, Bank Holiday fixtures, representative matches and Festivals was defined. The moralities were crystallised. 'Play up and play the game', 'It isn't cricket', became a code both implied and expressed and the county captains accepted responsibility for solving the problem of bowlers with suspect action.

In this development Yorkshire took a leading part. They were county champions in 1893, 1896 and 1898 and high in the list in years of interregnum. They gave players to England at home and abroad and sometimes raised comment by refusing to give players. With their success they also assumed a cloak of county character. 'Yorkshire cricket' came to have a specific interpretation.

In the last stage of their rise to fulfilment of ambition Yorkshire were not a settled team. They were both gathering and disposing of players. Louis Hall left the side in 1892, George Ulyett in 1893. Tunnicliffe came to join J. T. Brown and the amateur element of Arthur Sellers, Ernest Smith, F. S. Jackson, F. W. Milligan and Frank Mitchell was introduced. Wainwright came forward as bowler to take over 1,100 wickets and as batsman to score over 12,000 runs. A sturdily built young man named George Herbert Hirst earned his place as a persevering fast left-arm bowler with developing interests in batting.

Bobby Peel could fairly be considered the last of Yorkshire's 19th century cricketers. He was immensely talented as a player, firmly independent in character and susceptible to temptations in the way of life of professional cricketers of his time.

He came into the Yorkshire side, in 1882, when scope for his slow left-arm bowling was restricted because Peate was already established as a master in the same line of business. Yorkshire could indulge themselves because Peel, taking all his bowling opportunities, was also a batting asset and outstanding in the field. Before Peate's retirement Peel took 163 wickets for Yorkshire in five seasons. From 1888 to his own mid-season departure in 1897 Peel's bowling for his county brought 1,273 wickets. He was always master of his craft.

Competent batting gave him a double value to his county and country—Peel played in 20 matches for England—but he added to technical accomplishment an unquenchable enthusiasm for cricket. He was never a tired or dispirited bowler, never a reluctant batsman, never a fielder trying to avoid involvement.

Peel's career in first-class cricket ended on a peak of performance. In the season 1896 he scored 1,193 runs and took 108 wickets for Yorkshire. In the Oval Test of that year his bowling was decisive in England's victory over Australia when he took six wickets for 23 runs in the fourth innings.

In 1897 he mistimed indulgence in a secondary enthusiasm. One morning he was in no condition to appear on any cricket field and was bidden by his colleagues to stay out of sight—particularly out of sight of Lord Hawke, to whom he was reported as 'indisposed'. As Yorkshire went into the field with the 12th man, 12 men there were and one of them was Peel, expressing his readiness to bowl but proposing to do so with the pavilion rather than the stumps as a target.

The sequel was inevitable. Peel bore no grudge and lost no friend, but there was no longer a place for him in the new picture of Yorkshire cricket.

The Yorkshire built by Lord Hawke expressed unity nowhere better than in fielding and in this characteristic, at least, established an enduring county tradition. Yorkshire teams before 1890 were notoriously unreliable in the field, at one stage earning the rebuke that 'they were far too polite to run anyone out', but as they approached their glory they became famous for their fielding.

Some of the improvement no doubt resulted from improvement in the playing conditions. As pitches became more trustworthy under the influence of the heavy roller so did outfields. The ball could be picked up with more certainty and therefore returned with greater rapidity. Specialisation in positions developed, based on physical attributes and individual talents. Fielding acquired its own sphere of artistry until the exception in first-class cricket became not the good fielder but the poor one.

Amateur cricketers undoubtedly influenced the professionals. Some were more energetic than effective but youthful university players discovered in fielding their opportunity to equal and perhaps outstrip more mature and practised opponents. Professionals had to raise their standards, if only to preserve 'differentials'.

In the Yorkshire conception fielding competence became an essential and from competence brilliance developed. Ironically the ringmaster was perhaps the least accomplished, but Lord Hawke, whose catching was not infallible, was never an embarrassment to his side. He may have been less than great but he was certainly better than poor.

Yorkshire carried no 'passenger' fieldsmen and included several who developed fielding into an art with its own distinction. Tunnicliffe and Wainwright became famous in the slips, Wainwright for reliability, Tunnicliffe for astonishing range of activity.

Brown and Denton were specialists in the outfield, which was a busier sector than in present times because the basic principle of cricket's 'Golden Age' was challenge. Bowling was driven as much as it was deflected. Tunnicliffe's catches for Rhodes were, as often as not, from edged forcing shots; Denton's catches for Rhodes were from drives only slightly short of hits for six.

Long-off and long-on at one end became third man and deep fine leg at the other and Denton and Brown were as swift and accurate in pick-up and throw as they were sure in catching.

George Hirst guarded the gateway at mid-off. The position needed assurance and courage, for the off side was the general target of batting bombardment and the ball came to mid-off from the middle of the bat. Hirst was never known to flinch from the hardest hit, never known to make token gestures of interception. When the ball was skied within his range he had a rather unusual method of catching, with hands at eye-level instead of against the chest, but the outcome was rarely of benefit to the batsman.

The covers were for general patrol more than a specialist province. Wilfred Rhodes and Frank Mitchell and T. L. Taylor were to be found there and Rhodes became outstanding until he took up later residence in the slips to become characeristically effective in that position.

Rhodes was always a tremendous asset to a side in the field because he could fit in anywhere and never look out of place. The most professional of cricketers mastered fielding as professionally as he mastered bowling and batting.

Taylor was a wicketkeeper in his university days and kept wicket on a few occasions for Yorkshire, but he expressed thankfulness for limited opportunities. Keeping wicket to Yorkshire bowling demanded more than a willing heart. Taylor came to excellence in the field for self-protection, by his own confession. He told how, on one of his early appearances at Sheffield, a failure to pick up cleanly called forth the comment from the crowd, 'Nah then, tha ugly little black devil, tha'll have to do better than that.' The subject of reproof took heed; he improved his fielding that same afternoon and before he became Yorkshire President he had lost nearly all his black hair.

F. S. Jackson and Schofield Haigh were admirable in the field and so were most of the occasional players, in particular

Lees Whitehead, who played his first game for Yorkshire in 1889 and his last in 1904, was counted a regular member of the side in the later years, yet made few appearances. He was the accepted 12th man, useful as batsman and bowler, thoroughly reliable as substitute fieldsman.

In 1902, after Frank Mitchell had emigrated, a young left-hander was brought in to fill the batting vacancy. Irving Washington was an immediate success, completing his 1,000 runs and playing with such grace and skill that the brightest of futures seemed open to him, yet 1902 was his only full season in the first team. His health broke down and a cricketer of exceptional quality was lost to the county.

The focal point of an outstanding fielding side is always the wicketkeeper. Any shortcoming in him reflects on all; his skill can disguise weakness in detail that might otherwise become evident in colleagues.

David Hunter, who was Yorkshire's wicketkeeper for 21 years, found little need to cover up for his colleagues but had to maintain the highest standards in his own sphere to keep Yorkshire first in the field. He followed his elder brother Joe into the county side and when he came to retirement he had taken 965 catches and been awarded 372 stumpings. The figures may be taken as fair measure of legitimate achievement; Hunter rarely appealed without the assurance of conviction.

He was softly spoken, good-humoured and completely without a sense of self-importance. His praise was always for others and his murmured 'Well bowled, honey' was frequent tribute to the ball that beat the bat and missed the stumps. The full merit of his performances was often hidden by the admirable judgement that eliminated the need for spectacular acrobatics and so sure were his hands that all his long service brought little sign of injury or deformity.

Yorkshire's bowling asked more of him than most wicketkeepers are required to contrive. The allure of Rhodes gave sight of the ball as it turned away to the off, but Haigh's sharp breakback and Hirst's swerve across the batsmen's legs made successful positioning almost a magical art.

David Hunter contributed more to Yorkshire teams than wicketkeeping skill. He brought a serene temperament, a capacity for contentment that, in turn, brought him a lasting affection. When he retired from county cricket he was given public honour in the form of a banquet in his native Scarborough and for as long as he cared to attend he was always welcome on the cricket ground where his kindly help gave him the respect and adoration of schoolboys at practice.

Hunter made a supplementary name for himself as a last-wicket batsman. Mainly from that position in the order he scored more than 4,500 runs and with Lord Hawke he shared a 10th-wicket parnership of 148 against Kent in 1898. The runs were needed as were most of Hunter's runs. When times were easy Hunter's usual allotment was 'did not bat' or 'not out 0'.

4

Order of going in

Lord Hawke alone could not have created his chosen form of Yorkshire cricket. He conceived his ideal of a county team, he shaped it and he directed it in operation, but he was dependent on discovery of the appropriate constituents.

Yorkshire became a great team because the parts fitted together and held together. Individual talents were complementary, the spirit was common. The players knew their own functions and had confidence in the abilities of each other. Through the three triumphal seasons the representation was 'regular'. Of the 19 players appearing in 1900 five were substitutes of emergency, playing in fewer than five matches. In 1901 only 16 players were required, three of them fewer than five times. 1902 was a season of five Test matches against Australia and Yorkshire had to call on 20 players in the championship, though eight were no more than occasional members.

The regular team was not precisely the same for all three seasons. Wainwright retired at the end of 1901, leaving more room for Irving Washington, who played in 23 matches in 1902. The outstanding batsman of 1901 was the amateur Frank Mitchell, who emigrated to South Africa after that season. F. S. Jackson, because of military duties in the Boer War, played only in 1902.

The established players—the team—common to all three years comprised J. T. Brown, J. Tunnicliffe, D. Denton, G. H. Hirst, T. L. Tayor, Lord Hawke, W. Rhodes, S. Haigh and D. Hunter.

Taking their innings or going into the field they made a daunting prospect for any opponents.

Brown and Tunnicliffe were the opening batsmen. They first played together in 1891 when Tunnicliffe joined the side but they were not immediately brought into partnership.

Neither, indeed, could be said to have justified all batting expectations before 1893 when both scored 1,000 runs for the first time, but their affinity had been created by 1896 when the put up a century stand for the first wicket in both innings of the match against Middlesex at Lord's.

In 1897 they made 378 together against Sussex at Sheffield. In 1898 they raised the record to 554 against Derbyshire at Chesterfield. Through the great years they opened the innings by right of custom.

John Thomas Brown and John Tunnicliffe were partners in batting business and contrasts in appearance, personal character and style of play. Brown was small and stockily built and was a batsman of high ability and equally high self-confidence. The off side was his strength, with cutting his particular delight, and in normal circumstances he liked to lead the scoring in his partnership, but he had the technique to cope with the turning ball on a difficult pitch. He played eight times for England, touring Australia with A. E. Stoddart's team in 1894–5, heading the Test averages for the tourists and playing a memorable innings of 140 at Melbourne when England needed 297 to win match and rubber.

In his youthful days Brown fielded brilliantly in the deep. Later he made the gully or point his recognised station in a team of fielding distinction and specialisation. He left cricket, in 1904, through ill-health and died towards the end of that year at the age of 45.

John Tunnicliffe was lean and uncommonly tall and nicknamed 'Long John of Pudsey'. As a young batsman his inclination was to hit the ball as hard and as often as possible, but he found, at county level, that unrestrained adventure was unprofitable and he became predominantly defensive in outlook and method.

The self-control was typical. Tunnicliffe could be a careful batsman because he was a careful man, imbued with the strongest sense of loyalty and social conscience. Tunnicliffe was essentially and contentedly a county cricketer, and Yorkshire was his county. He had immense respect for himself, for Lord Hawke and for the cricket made available to him. He was austere but not bigoted, serious-minded but not without all sense of humour. He was a sobering influence but not a wet blanket.

Tunnicliffe's batting distinction derived from achievements in partnership. Brown and Tunnicliffe became a famous pair. Tunnicliffe added a secondary reputation in cricket on the individual basis of his fielding in the slips.

His great height was both an asset and a liability. It meant that his preliminary position had to be in the nature of a straddle with feet wide apart to provide the crouch necessary to cope with the low ball. Tall men can rise more quickly than they can stoop, so Tunnicliffe set himself in the stooping position. The disadvantage is sideways immobility. From the stoop a swift step to right or left is virtually impossible and Tunnicliffe, of necessity, moved sideways, or upwards, in the form of a leap. Long arm outstretched, he covered an enormous range and the record books credit him with 678 catches. He was, of course, well supplied with material. The cricket of his time was an off-side game and Peel and Rhodes were artists in finding the edge of the bat.

Of the 19 century opening partnerships shared by Brown and Tunnicliffe, two were colossal. In 1897 they put on 378 against Sussex at Sheffield; in 1898 they reached 554 against Derbyshire at Chesterfield.

The 378 was a record for its time; the 554 long outlived its generation.

It was made in the context of the match and in unlikely circumstances. The Chesterfield ground was being used for the first time in county championship fixtures and the match had been allocated to William Sugg as a benefit.

When Yorkshire won the toss and took first innings Tunnicliffe was a hungry man, not metaphorically for runs—he was enjoying an excellent season—but literally for food. Because of confused arrangements he had missed his evening meal on the previous day and he had also missed a night's sleep because he feared dampness in the bed offered by an unsatisfactory lodging.

He missed breakfast to catch an early train and after batting through to lunchtime he found that the players were compelled to take their chance with the spectators in the refreshment tent. Tunnicliffe's achievement was one small sandwich.

Lord Hawke's comments on the catering provision for his 'boys' would have been interesting, as would his reactions on the batting from a personal inconvenience. His Lordship had decided to go in first-wicket down.

County rules made no provision for a tea interval at that period of cricket, but with Brown and Tunnicliffe still together at an appropriate hour the mercy of an interval was needed, proposed and agreed. Lord Hawke took his pads off for the day. He would not in any case have required them; Brown and Tunnicliffe were not out at close of play.

On the second morning Yorkshire's batting instructions were to hit away without regard for consequences (declaration being outside the law) and the first wicket pair added some 60 runs in little more than quarter of an hour before Tunnicliffe was caught at slip for 243. Brown reached 300 and deliberately hit wicket. Yorkshire reached 662 and won by an innings and 387 runs.

Lord Hawke was Yorkshire's frustrated No. 3 at Chesterfield, but that place in the batting was customarily allotted to David Denton, whose county career stretched from 1894 to 1920. He was a brilliant batsman, probably deprived of international distinction only by the greater brilliance of his contemporary, J. T. Tyldesley. Tyldesley played 31 times for England, Denton only 11, and most of those appearances were in South Africa when Tyldesley was not in the touring team.

Tyldesley's advantage over Denton lay in his superiority against the turning ball. In most other aspects of cricketing talent the two were gifted in parallel. Both adventured from the prose into the poetry of batting. Both gleamed with polish in the off-side strikes. Both scored rapidly and heavily, claiming an aggregate of more than 2,000 runs in five seasons. Both were rated high among the principal batting attractions of their time and both added the distinction of famous fielding.

Denton's ability was remarked on his first appearance for Yorkshire in 1894 and in the following season he established his position. He came at the time when Yorkshire cricketers were acquiring the financial stability and unity of purpose Lord Hawke so much desired for them and in the great years Denton was one of the great players.

He fitted admirably into the Yorkshire side as batsman, replacing Ulyett in rapid scoring and as fieldsman succeeding Wainwright as a specialist in the deep. Because of his characteristic enterprise, which began with the beginning of his innings, he flirted with fate more than most leading batsmen and he was rather unkindly labelled as 'Lucky Denton' on grounds that he enjoyed more than his fair share of 'lives' in the slips. His retort could have been 33,608 runs and a murmur that edged drives are harder to catch than edged defensive strokes.

In the outfield Denton was acknowledged to be without peer. He had speed, he had judgement and his catching was so remarkably safe than an error by him was a feature not only of a match but of a whole season.

The major batting contributions of Yorkshire's amateurs came from T. L. Taylor and, in 1901, F. Mitchell. Both came to county cricket, like Lord Hawke, with Cambridge University experience and both were good enough to lead the Yorkshire averages, Mitchell with 1,674 runs in 1901, Taylor with an aggregate of 1,276 in 1902.

Both left Yorkshire cricket to their own and to Yorkshire's regret. Mitchell emigrated to South Africa, visiting England as captain of the South African touring team in 1904. Taylor, for whom the Yorkshire captaincy was clearly designated, had to put aside his cricket after 1902 to meet demands of a family business.

Mitchell was a hard-hitting batsman, noted for powerful straight driving, but centuries in four successive championship matches in 1901 indicate enterprise under control. Taylor's consistent success was based on a fighting spirit and uncommon powers of concentration when batting conditions were difficult.

Mitchell, like F. S. Jackson, was taken away from two of the three historic seasons because of the Boer War. Taylor fitted perfectly into the Yorkshire scheme of supremacy and came as near to an England 'cap' as being among the 12 invited to the Lord's Test of 1902.

The amateurs, who included Ernest Smith, a schoolmaster available in the later part of the season, contributed more than their playing ability to the Yorkshire strength of the time. Their presence undoubtedly added to Lord Hawke's pleasures of cricket and thus to his deep and continuing interest. By the customs of the period amateurs and professionals carried different social obligations. They did not stay together during away matches, they did not usually occupy the same dressing-room. Without some amateur companionship Lord Hawke would probably have found his summers less congenial and his incentive to play less strong.

5

His Excellency

F. S. Jackson was the most gifted of all Yorkshire's amateur cricketers. Birthright into comfortable financial and social circumstances gave him opportunity to develop his talent at Harrow School and Cambridge University and as an undergraduate he became an England cricketer. To any suggestion that the kissing of selection might have gone by social favour Jackson replied with an innings of 91 in his first Test and 103 in his second. He did not play in the third and last Test of that series—Yorkshire persuaded him to Brighton for a critical match in the county championship!

Circumstances that made Jackson available to cricket also took him away from it. He undertook military service and political service in the tradition of his family, thereby missing tours, whole seasons of English cricket and coming to premature retirement from the first-class field. In exchange he became Colonel the Hon. Sir Stanley Jackson, P.C., G.C.I.E., sometime Financial Secretary to the War Office and Governor of Bengal.

At all times he looked his part and nowhere more so than on the cricket field. He was immaculate in the costume of his day, which included a coloured sash at the waist both for decorative and practical purposes. He had the dignified assurance of supreme self-confidence derived from training and controlled temperament. As a cricketer he did not so much overcome crisis as ignore it and it was characteristic that when, as Governor of Bengal, he suffered attempted assassination he should brush the alarm aside as though an incident of no more than momentary concern.

In the high offices of his later life, President of M.C.C., President of Yorkshire, battalion commander, he flavoured all his authority with diplomacy and tactful forethought. He won his battles by persuasion as distinct from storm. He saw through complications to the essential simplicities. After an M.C.C. committee had conducted long debate on suitable wording for the memorial gates to W. G. Grace at Lord's, Jackson's quiet recommendation was: 'Why not—The Great Cricketer?'

F. S. Jackson shared in the approach to Yorkshire's peak years, scoring his 1,000 county runs in every season from 1896 to 1899 and taking 240 wickets in those years, but he did not play in any championship match of 1900 and 1901. In 1902 he returned from war to cricket and was characteristically successful, but England wanted him for the five Tests against Australia, the Gentlemen and other representative sides wanted him as often as they could get him and Yorkshire were without him in 10 of their 25 championship games.

Jackson was, therefore, almost a supernumary in the teams of triumph, yet no player could have represented more appropriately the amateur approach and the Yorkshire approach to the cricket of the period. He played cricket because he enjoyed the game and could afford indulgence in the pastime, but he was not prepared to play on terms of sufferance by his peers. He never played at playing.

He brought to his principal recreation all the skill, all the experience, all the concentration at his disposal. His attitude to games as he desired them for himself was perfectly illustrated when he turned, after his cricketing days, to golf. He applied himself to this new interest through a winter of study, instruction and development of technique. Then he went on to the course and within a year was rated at scratch. To him the challenge of a game was the challenge to ability.

Jackson's cricketing ability was to be measured in superlatives. None of his contemporaries questioned his quality, no historian has sought to diminish his standing. His career glittered with achievement as batsman and bowler in statistical terms alone. In 20 Test matches, all against Australia, he scored 1,412 runs, completing five centuries. In 1905 he headed the England batting averages, the England bowling averages and captained the winning side in the series. In Yorkshire's records he stands among the few who have scored over 10,000 runs and taken over 500 wickets.

Spectacular results were not achieved by ostentatious manner of play. Jackson's cricketing methods were as neat and conventional as was his personal appearance. He was rather above average height though not noticeably tall, slim and beautifully coordinated in movement.

His batting contained no peculiarity of stroke, no emphasis on any one shot, no virtue applicable to special circumstances. He played in the orthodox mould and played with impressive technique and judgement.

Perhaps the most difficult of the textbook batting strokes to play flawlessly is the on-drive because it requires such accurate combination of positioning, balance and timing. Jackson played the on-drive with rare facility, but he was not bound by it and he did not embarrass himself to contrive it. His batsmanship was comprehensive. He accepted each ball as it came, watched it with infinite care and produced his counter-stroke from a wide range.

He was neither a hitter nor a defender. He needed no particular type of pitch nor of bowling to display his talent in the best light.

As a bowler he exhibited the same qualities of inborn ability developed by painstaking command of technique. He bowled gracefully, without flourish or any extravagance of effort in run-up and right-arm delivery. His pace was rather above medium with occasional slower off-break, or off-cutter, as variation and accuracy of length and direction was his strength.

Lord Hawke reports an occasion when Yorkshire were playing Surrey at Bradford in which circumstances demanded a check to the Surrey rate of scoring. Jackson bowled several impeccable overs before making a mistake in direction that permitted an easy run to be taken. At the end of the over Jackson went to his captain, 'I'm awfully sorry,' he said. He had fallen from his standard of perfection.

The more important the match, the sterner became Jackson's resolution. His Test-match averages were an improvement on his county averages. He rarely failed when Yorkshire were playing Lancashire and when Yorkshire met the Australians in 1902 he supported Hirst in bowling them out for a first innings total of 23.

All his five centuries for England were made under pressure of need for a batting recovery and innumerable innings for Yorkshire were played to change the course of a match or determine its outcome. Perhaps more than any cricketer of his time he was assured of a welcome into any team for which he could make himself available. At the Scarborough Festival of 1900 he made his one appearance of the season—home on leave from the Boer War—and hasty placards were published: 'F. S. Jackson Will Definitely Play.'

He did; and scored 134.

6

Mastery

In 1900 Yorkshire came to consummation of the glory they had been approaching for a decade. They won the championship by playing through a programme of 28 matches with 16 victories and not a single defeat. These results gave them a percentage of 100 by the system that awarded a point for victory, deducted a point for defeat and ignored drawn games.

Yorkshire were masterfully successful. Six of their victories were by an innings, two were by 10 wickets and their narrowest margin of success was 40 runs. They opened their programme with sensation and completed it with triumph heaped on triumph.

The first match against Worcestershire at Bradford, occupied only one day. In early May the pitches were soft and the ball would turn. Worcestershire, batting first, were put out by Rhodes and Haigh, bowling unchanged for 43. Yorkshire scored 99 and Rhodes and Haigh bowled again to dismiss Worcestershire for 51 in an hour's cricket.

An August match, at Harrogate, also brought astonishing victory in little more than a day. After some two and a half hours' cricket on the first day and none at all on the second, the morning scoreboard on the last day—which was a Saturday—showed Yorkshire at 159 for nine wickets. They were all out for 171. Essex were harried and hurried to the destruction of 65, Rhodes taking six wickets. Yorkshire were satisfied with declaration at 42 for one, leaving time for Essex to be put out again, this time for 52, Rhodes demanding eight wickets in 13 overs.

Possibility of defeat came Yorkshire's way at Bradford, though in the end they won by 40 runs. They were comfortably placed with 409 to Gloucestershire's 269 in first innings and certainly not in anxiety when Gloucestershire were set 327 to make in the last innings. True, Jessop could never be discounted, but Jessop had made 104 in 65 minutes in the first innings and lightning is supposed not to strike twice in the same place.

This lightning did. Coming in halfway down the order Jessop hit Rhodes for seven sixes and scored 139 in an hour and a half.

Yorkshire's authority of 1900 was enhanced in 1901 when the championship was taken with 20 victories from 27 matches. One defeat was suffered and it was the sensation of the season because it came like thunderstorm from a clear sky in mid-season after a sequence of 17 matches contained 15 victories and two draws. Most of the victories had been overwhelming, seven of them with an innings to spare, and when Somerset came to Leeds on July 15 the fixture carried no more than routine significance.

The first day's play followed anticipation. Somerset were dismissed for 87. When Yorkshire had scored 325 Somerset preceded their second innings with precautionary travel reservations for the evening of the second day. They had to be cancelled. Somerset were still batting at close of play. Palairet had made a century, Braund had made a century, Phillips had made a century and Yorkshire's bowling had been cut, carved and driven to helplessness.

When the innings ended on the third morning, for a total of 630, only Rhodes dared to contemplate the bowling analysis and his return was six wickets for 145 runs.

Fourth-innings requirement was far beyond Yorkshire's reach. Had their spirit permitted them to attempt nearly 400 runs conditions would have been prohibitive. The pitch had broken up and Yorkshire were all out for 113.

This solitary lapse of the season was a paradoxical measure of Yorkshire's greatness and of their reputation. It meant nothing in the championship and claimed its place in cricket history as contrast to Yorkshire's typical conquests. The essence of the drama was not Somerset success but Yorkshire failure. Somerset did win other matches. Yorkshire were beaten only once in two years—and were to lose only twice in three years.

Yorkshire success had ceased to be astonishing but some of

the achievements of 1901 carried more than passing remark. At Trent Bridge Nottinghamshire were dismissed for 13. At Leyton Yorkshire won by an innings and 33 runs with a total of 104. Essex made 30 and 41. Opponents were dismissed for under 100 on 15 occasions. Yorkshire's total exceeded 400 six times, five of them producing an innings victory.

1902 brought Yorkshire equally decisively to the top of the championship table. In a wet summer their opportunity to complete matches was reduced and their record contained 11 draws and 13 victories, but again they were only once defeated —and again by Somerset. In the drawn matches they seemed in little danger of defeat, save perhaps by Sussex at Brighton.

Somerset, advantageously winning the toss on a soft pitch, outplayed them at Sheffield in a low-scoring match that was dominated by the batting and bowling of L. C. Braund, but as adequate compensation Lancashire were dismissed for 72 and 54 and defeated with an innings to spare. Middlesex were not permitted to total 100 in any of their four completed innings of the home and away games and in seven successive fixtures during May and June Yorkshire never had to field through an innings exceeding 129.

Yorkshire's county championship record for the three seasons of 1900, 1901, 1902 reads:

Played	Won	Lost	Drawn
80	59	2	29

In their success Yorkshire experienced the reactions commonly raised by success. They were applauded for their efforts, they were admired for their achievement and as they consolidated their position of superiority they began to lose some affection.

Yorkshire in 1902 were a less popular team than Yorkshire in 1900 simply because of their continuing success. They did, inevitably, undergo some change in character. Rare defeat tends to make defeat more intolerable. Success breeding success can lead to an isolation, a difference in outlook, that might be interpreted in terms of arrogance. There comes a stage when it is almost not 'sporting' to win too readily or too often.

Yorkshire matches did undoubtedly begin to lose some flavour, not because Yorkshire won too well but because their cricketing superiority of the period invested opposition with some inclination towards despair and consequent disinterest. Yorkshire themselves could do nothing about that. They could only play to the best of their ability. They could scarcely be expected to apologise for winning or for making conquest their continual and urgent concern.

From the three-year domination grew a long-lasting tradition that Yorkshire viewed cricket differently from other counties, that Yorkshire played essentially to win, that cricket was not played 'for fun' by Yorkshiremen, that Yorkshire cricket had a 'hardness', effective but not necessarily enviable.

Yorkshire cricket certainly acquired an individuality. It was recognisable by more than a cap with a white rose. It came to be regarded as the cricket of a close community, cricket expressed in terms of high self-confidence, cricket of technical excellence moulded and devoted to a team purpose. Cricketers from Yorkshire underwent a subtle metamorphosis into Yorkshire cricketers.

On occasions county was put before country and the county club won few friends for such insistence. As far back as 1893 Middlesex had raised disapproving eyebrows when they found Wainwright in the side opposing them after the county committee had reported him unavailable for an England team. In 1901 Hirst and Rhodes were invited to join A. C. Maclaren's team touring Australia, but Yorkshire, on Lord Hawke's recommendation, withheld permission.

This overriding authority was illustration of Lord Hawke's Yorkshire. His cricketers were 'his men', inspired and required to exchange the freelance attitude of the 19th-century professional player for closer loyalty deriving from county community. Lord Hawke insisted on the loyalty but he commanded it through his personal inspiration and through his unceasing concern for the welfare of those who followed him.

Hirst and Rhodes received financial compensation for missing an Australian tour and there was, in fact, a principle involved in the ban. Lord Hawke was prime mover in the demand for official sponsorship of Tests at home and tours abroad. Once a Board of Control had been created and M.C.C. had made themselves responsible for overseas tours Yorkshire became the readiest of co-operators in release of players for national needs. Lord Hawke was prepared to make his players available to constitutional establishment because he was assured that the players would then be safeguarded by the same sense of responsibility shown by Yorkshire. Lord Hawke liked his own way and his own way was the way to welfare for others.

7

Bowled—Hirst, Haigh or Rhodes

Yorkshire's strength in their most powerful periods was in all-round equipment. They could bat, they could bowl and they could field, but all cricket history shows that bowling and fielding are the decisive factors in county championships and Test-match rubbers. Batting sets the dining table, but bowling and fielding cook the goose of cricketing opposition.

Yorkshire in the 1900-2 period of conquest had wonderful bowling resources. They had fast bowling, orthodox in the presentation by Ernest Smith when he joined the side during school holidays, but unusual in the particular manner of George Hirst. They had medium-pace from F. S. Jackson and Schofield Haigh. They had slow left-arm spin from Wilfred Rhodes.

Wainwright's most effective bowling days were in an earlier decade, but he took a few wickets with his prodigious off-break in 1900 and 1901. J. T. Brown bowled occasionally, offering slow, high-flighted 'donkey drops', as they were called, to induce embarrassing mishits and another J. T. Brown, known as 'Darfield Brown' to distinguish him from his senior namesake, gave promise as a fast bowler until a shoulder injury cut short his career.

In Jackson's absence the bowling strength was essentially the strength of George Herbert Hirst, Schofield Haigh and Wilfred Rhodes. It was more than adequate. Frequently only three Yorkshire bowlers appeared in a match analysis, sometimes only two.

In 1900 Rhodes and Haigh shared 351 of the 452 wickets taken in the championship fixtures. In 1901 Rhodes and Hirst claimed 331 of 447; in 1902 Rhodes and Haigh 263 of 352. (The figures exclude run out and negligible returns of 'also bowled'.)

Wilfred Rhodes was the factor common in all success. No

cricketer in the whole history of the game can claim figures comparable with his in the first five seasons of a bowling career. Playing his first Yorkshire match in the spring of 1898, Rhodes had taken 1,058 wickets at summer's end in 1902. In first-class cricket Rhodes never served an apprenticeship; he came as a master-craftsman, his talent beyond question, his technique already polished.

Schofield Haigh came less dramatically to renown and he changed his bowling to meet requirements and extend his abilities. Like Hirst and Rhodes, he was a native of the Huddersfield district and in his early days of professional cricket he was a fast bowler, taking an unusually long run up.

Figures show that he was an effective fast bowler but he became an exceptional bowler by shortening his run, reducing his pace and concentrating on the control of a lively off-break. The remains of his fast-bowling approach were to be seen in a long delivery stride that carried the front foot to the popping crease and sometimes dragged the back foot through the bowling crease.

Haigh was on the shorter side of average height and the long swing of his bowling arm, the right arm, which began from behind his back, gave his flight a rather low trajectory. From this a slower ball, usually designed to be a yorker, became difficult to judge and batsmen were deceived into anticipating a full toss. On soft turf his sharp off-break was devastating and he frequently bowled round the wicket to give himself more scope for hitting the stumps.

Haigh was not an all-rounder in the sense that his batting ranked equally with his bowling in service to his team, but he was far from helpless at the crease. He scored 11,099 Yorkshire runs and in 1904 he reached 1,000 runs and took 100 wickets. Opportunities for long inning were limited, but he has four centuries to his name and he was never to be included among inconsequential tail-enders. With characteristic good humour he once came to the wicket and informed the fielding side that he had 'brought the key'. Asked to explain himself Haigh said, 'The key of the hutch—we have only rabbits left'—and then

Lord Hawke, who captained Yorkshire for 27 seasons and was President for 40 years

ABOVE LEFT Edward Peate, who averaged five wickets a match during his eight-year career

ABOVE RIGHT F. S. Jackson, the greatest of Yorkshire's amateurs

BELOW The Yorkshire side of 1875

ABOVE LEFT George Ulyett, who was known as 'Happy Jack'
ABOVE RIGHT Robert Peel, who came into the Yorkshire side in 1882
BELOW LEFT J. Tunnicliffe, who was nicknamed 'Long John of Pudsey'
BELOW RIGHT G. Freeman, who played for the county between 1865 and 1881

J. T. Brown, who toured Australia under A. E. Stoddart in 1894–5

The 1902 Yorkshire team. From left to right, back row, I. Washington, D. Hunter, J. Tunnicliffe, L. Whitehead, W. Rhodes. Middle, G. H. Hirst, F. S. Jackson, Lord Hawke (capt.), T. L. Taylor, S. Haigh. Front, J. T. Brown, D. Denton settled in to share a century partnership with Tunnicliffe who had been holding the fort through a collapse.

Haigh probably received less than his deserts in recognition at international level. He toured South Africa twice but played in only four home Tests, all against Australia. In Yorkshire's records he has a long list of 'Notable Bowling Performances', ranging from eight for 33 against Warwickshire in 1898 to six for 14 against the 1912 Australians. He took nine wickets in an innings against Gloucestershire, bowled unchanged through an innings three times with Rhodes and twice with Hirst and he did the hat-trick three times.

That he should share bowling distinction with Hirst, as he also shared batting distinction in a county ninth-wicket partnership of 192, was appropriate. Haigh had an immense respect and affection for Hirst, who was his senior in cricket though not in years. In the inevitable associations that grow in teams Haigh linked himself firmly to Hirst. They should have gone together on a coaching engagement to India but the death of the sponsoring maharajah cancelled the undertaking and in 1913 Haigh left first-class cricket to become a coach at Winchester College.

Haigh had the sunniest of dispositions and extracted all possible enjoyment from his cricketing life. He was never downhearted in difficulty or despondent in defeat and he met the implication of approaching end to his Yorkshire career with his broadest smile. With Hirst (of course) he was entering the ground at Bath. 'Umpires?' questioned the gateman. 'Yes,' replied Haigh, and walked on to the players' dressing-room.

Haigh's hero, George Hirst, also came to Yorkshire with the credentials of a promising fast bowler. So he remained for a few seasons, the promise maturing and batting ability rapidly developing through observation and practice. By 1893, five seasons after his first county appearance, Hirst was collecting his 100 wickets and by 1896 he was capable of making 1,000 runs as well. A sturdy cricketer, bowling left-handed and batting right-handed and fielding with unflagging energy and courage, had established himself as a 'good companion' among colleagues and spectators alike.

Towards the turn of the century Hirst began to develop skills that placed him in a category of his own in cricket. He cultivated the 'George Hirst Swerve' and the 'George Hirst Pull'.

The swerve was a logical consequence of his natural form of delivery and thoughtful calculation. Hirst had a bounding run-up—to bowl round the wicket—and a loose, easy action in which the left arm was not taken over at maximum height. The course of flight would be from the outside edge of the bowling crease, or wider, towards the leg-side.

Hirst noticed that when he bowled a yorker the ball sometimes followed a line down the off-side and curved suddenly in the later stages of its flight. He observed the conditions most favourable to this peculiarity, experimented with the grip of the ball and the placing of his feet in the delivery stride. He commanded the swerve, where earlier he had executed it virtually by accident.

This accomplishment transformed his bowling. Without the swerve he would have remained a fine bowler, because length and direction were basic principles and he had lively pace and a breakback. With the swerve he became a phenomenon.

George Hirst's swerve was not precisely calculable by either George Hirst or the bewildered batsman. On what he called his 'funny days' the ball might come to the bat like a good return from cover-point, as one victim proclaimed, or drift across the pads to be edged into the leg-trap. On other days, or when the ball lost shine and seam, the swerve disappeared as suddenly as morning mist under a hot sun. One set of circumstances provided bowling figures verging on the ridiculous; another set meant an analysis reflecting hours of determined attack. Any set meant the certainty was that the bowler would be trying his hardest. Because he tried and never gave up George Hirst won the heart of all cricketers.

In batting Hirst began at the bottom and worked himself steadily to his 1,000 and sometimes 2,000 runs a season by applying what he had observed and by inspiring himself with the bold spirit that considered no cause lost and no challenge beyond meeting. He played all the orthodox strokes and then added a daring pull—not a sweep with horizontal bat—that took the good-length ball from the middle stump and hastened it to, or beyond, the mid-wicket boundary. The risk was calculated; George Hirst was l.b.w. often enough but he filled the scorebook with boundaries.

Hirst could have played in the highest company as a batsman without being a bowler or as a bowler without being a batsman, but nobody would have claimed him as either the greatest batsman or the greatest bowler of his time. Almost everybody did acclaim him as the most beloved cricketer ever to step on the field.

George Hirst had a warmth, a kindliness, a spirit of endeavour that communicated itself from pitch to boundary line. He thrilled by the manner of his doing as much as by his deeds. His rescue innings, his bowling spells of conquest, his fearless fielding at mid-off swelled the heart with vicarious pride and the mind with wonder. George Hirst was the cricketer all cricketers wanted to be when they idealised themselves. His technical accomplishments were, no doubt, far beyond the general understanding, but the earnestness, the vigour, the good humour, the affection with which he played were for universal appreciation and admiration.

George Hirst always seemed to be precisely what he was—a cricketer playing with pleasure to give pleasure and when stumps were drawn for the day he enjoyed his pipe and his pint.

8

Benefit taken

After playing 80 championship matches in three seasons and experiencing only two defeats Yorkshire could scarcely expect to continue at such heights of achievement. Some players maintained or even increased their skills, but others in the natural course of events passed their peak or dropped out of cricket through injury, illness or because of overriding personal commitments.

In 1903 nothing was seen of T. L. Taylor, who was engaged in family business. 'Darfield' Brown, the fast bowler, suffered the dislocated shoulder that ended his career. Washington was unavailable through illness and though George Hirst eventually completed his double of 1,000 runs and 100 wickets and headed both batting and bowling averages, a knee injury in May severely limited the amount of bowling he could undertake.

Yorkshire's power was reduced, but there was certainly no descent to a place among the weaker counties. They were third in the championship in 1903, second in 1904 and, rather surprisingly to themselves, first again in 1905.

By this time the association of Brown and Tunnicliffe had been ended by Brown's enforced retirement and 1905 was a year of Australian Tests, for which Jackson was required five times (as England captain), Rhodes four times, Hirst three, Haigh twice and Denton once. County vacancies offered opportunity for extended experience to Rothery as an opening batsman and to Myers and Ringrose as bowlers. Rothery scored 738 runs in championship matches, Myers took 62 wickets and Ringrose 60, all justifying their inclusion though none in the end was able to fulfil the highest expectations.

In 1905 the championship system contained a complication that led Yorkshire into a remarkable performance against

Essex at Leyton near the end of the season. Outright defeat would have meant a steep fall in percentage; a drawn match cost nothing.

Batting first to score 521 Essex virtually eliminated one of the possible results, but as their innings had extended far into the second morning and pitch and weather showed no sign of deterioration a drawn game seemed a probable outcome.

In the dramatic second afternoon a young cricketer playing in his first county season did the hat-trick and found himself with five wickets to his name after three overs. The name was Douglas and his initials, which became equally well known, were J.W.H.T.

Yorkshire were all out for 98. An evening hour and a whole day stretched before them, with survival the only purpose in their follow-on batting. They survived: Tunnicliffe and Hirst for three hours and 15 minutes in partnership; Hirst for nearly five hours over the incidental collection of 90 runs; Ernest Smith an hour for 0 not out. Essex bowled 150 overs to take seven wickets.

In the 1905 season Yorkshire fielded to one other total of over 400. This was at Leicester where C. J. B. Wood and S. Coe completed centuries in the Leicestershire 419. Yorkshire had lost three wickets for 22 runs when Hirst came to the crease, where he stayed for seven hours to hit one six and 53 fours in Yorkshire's record individual innings of 341.

Years later Hirst's recollection of the occasion was characteristic. 'I remember,' he said, 'the fielding of a substitute, Tom Jayes, who saved boundary after boundary and got more applause for stopping runs than I did for scoring them.'

Before his record score Hirst had already acquired another Yorkshire record. In 1904 his benefit match had been played.

Lancashire helpfully changed the fixtures so that Yorkshire could be at home, at Headingley, over the August Bank Holiday weekend. The circumstances were ideal. Lancashire were an unbeaten side, the weather over all three days was gloriously fine, the match was taken to a draw, with Yorkshire in general advantage, George Hirst was a public idol.

Attendances were 31,826, 31,579 and 15,387. When expenses had been deducted from gate receipts and subscriptions Hirst was left with £3,703, and 20 years passed, with intervening devaluations of war, before that amount was exceeded as a cricketer's reward.

The benefit match was an age-old feature of professional cricket and Yorkshire players have, on the whole, been well and justly rewarded, but the system contains inherent weaknesses of chance. Match appeal and weather cannot be arranged. Grounds vary widely in attendance capacity. Response is dependent not only on personal factors but on the significance of cricket in the area.

More general practice of the present day, when few county matches carry much margin of receipts over expenditure, is to allocate a year for collections and fund-raising without dependence on a specific match occasion and to provide some form of endowment assurance.

Under Lord Hawke's guidance Yorkshire instituted trustees for benefit funds, setting aside as much as two-thirds of the proceeds for family safeguard in the future. The principle has raised anomalies, sometimes manifestly serving its purpose, sometimes creating unintended complications that have not been appreciated by the players.

Whatever their feelings no Yorkshire players have refused benefit or the alternative grants, though one did accumulate dividend warrants for years without cashing them, in his insistence that the county's trustee rules were operating unfairly.

9

Toll of time

In the seasons from 1906 to 1914 Yorkshire won the championship twice, were second three times and had two disappointing experiences when they fell to eighth position in 1910 and seventh in 1911.

The lowly years were a regretful admission of the march of time and the incomplete fulfilment of promise. Lord Hawke gave up the captaincy, Tunnicliffe and Hunter had gone, Haigh was approaching the end and policy decided to accept cloud overhead for bright prospect on the horizon.

Reconstruction had been foreshadowed, for the championship success of 1908 represented a burst of flame rather than a growing fire of accomplishment. 1907 had not promised great things for 1908; it had been a season of dismal weather, a whole month passing without a match completed in the Yorkshire programme; a season in which John Tunnicliffe had sent in a characteristically courteous resignation on being offered a coaching appointment; a season in which the future batting and bowling support for Hirst, Rhodes, Haigh and Denton was not evident.

Hirst and Rhodes remained colossal in cricket, Rhodes reaching the top of the batting ladder he had always proposed to climb and taking a season's 100 wickets when necessary, almost as makeweight. Hirst touched incredibility with 2,000 runs and 200 wickets in 1906 and went on scoring 1,000 runs and taking 100 wickets in every season to 1913.

For all that, Hirst in 1908 became 37 years old before the end of the season and fast bowlers at 37 begin to feel some protest from their legs. Yorkshire were not hoping to find another Hirst, or Rhodes; they were hoping to find players of adequacy to help Hirst and Rhodes and capable of learning from mastery still in mastery.

1908 brought more help than could reasonably have been expected. Hirst took 164 wickets, Rhodes 100, Haigh 93 and J. T. Newstead took 131. Newstead had been known to Yorkshire since 1903, but not as a bowler, and in his few appearances his batting had not been notably successful. By 1907 he was still filling occasional vacancies and in that capacity he was playing against Worcestershire when he took seven wickets for 10 runs.

In 1908, in his 29th year, he developed beyond belief. His right-arm fast-medium bowling acquired a liveliness and accuracy that made him a sensation of the season. Yorkshire passed through their championship programme undefeated, winning 16 matches and had there been a Test match Newstead would in all probability have won an England cap.

He never came within consideration. By 1909 the magic had left his bowling. He struggled to take 80 expensive wickets and in three more years he had faded entirely from the county scene.

After 1908, when the championship was taken without a defeat, the graph of efficiency showed a continuation of descent. By the spring of 1911 it had become obvious that the supporting players were not likely to develop into the leaders now becoming urgently necessary. It was time for cutting losses and investing in new talent.

Lord Hawke, who had appeared little in 1909 and even less in 1910, formally resigned the captaincy. Hunter had retired in 1909 and Arthur Dolphin had established himself in the wicketkeeping succession. Myers and Rothery were not re-engaged for 1911 and both batting and bowling places were made available to any young players promising the desired skill and temperament.

Two immediate satisfactions were recorded. From Sheffield —through the county second team—came Alonzo Drake and from Pudsey, also through the Colts, came M. W. Booth, whose Christian names were Major William.

Both were all-rounders, Drake left-handed and Booth right-handed. Booth was a fast-medium bowler, Drake medium-pace. Their ability was reflected in performances. Both reached their 1,000 runs in 1911 and 1913. Booth took more than 100 wickets in 1912, 1913 and 1914, Drake in 1913 and 1914. Booth twice did the hat-trick and so did Drake, his second achievement extending to four wickets in four balls. Together they bowled unchanged through the two innings of matches against Gloucestershire and Somerset in 1914.

The development of Booth and Drake no doubt contributed, through easing of the burden of responsibility, to the continuing success of senior players. Hirst and Rhodes could reduce the number of overs they had to bowl, probably to the benefit of their batting. In the six seasons from 1909 to 1914 Hirst scored 9,228 runs, Rhodes 10,757 in his established capacity as opening batsman. His recognised partner from 1911 was B. B. Wilson, from Scarborough, who disappointed only in his seeming reluctance to decimate bowling he had already mastered.

David Denton enjoyed a wonderful season in 1912 when he made six centuries and scored 2,088 Yorkshire runs. This was not his biggest county aggregate, but it was remarkable in an exceptionally wet summer. Mainly because of Denton's batting and the soft pitches serving the eager and varied bowling Yorkshire won the championship.

This success must have been a special gratification to Sir Archibald White in the first season of a captaincy he held until the outbreak of war. Neither White nor E. J. Radcliffe, who was immediate successor to Lord Hawke, would have claimed for himself first-class standards of cricket, but both came forward in response to a need of the time and were rewarded with happy recollections of the loyalty and practical advice offered to them by the senior professionals.

County cricket in 1914 ended without cricketers' hearts in it. The championship continued after the declaration of war, Kent finishing at the top of the table, with Yorkshire in fourth place, but such improvisations as Surrey *v.* Yorkshire at Lord's because the Oval had been commandeered created an air of unreality and cancellation of the end-of-season Festivals implied more than the end of a programme.

10

Ends and beginnings

In the gallery of Yorkshire portraits the 1919 team photograph marks the beginning of a new section; should, indeed, introduce a new alcove.

Gone from the cricketing company are Major Booth, Alonzo Drake and B. B. Wilson; gone Sir Archibald White and the T. J. Birtles who was finding his feet as a batsman at first-class level in 1914.

Booth was killed in the Somme slaughter of 1916. Drake was warned of poor health by rejection from military service and he died in the spring of 1919. Wilson at the age of 39 was considered unlikely to advance further and Birtles at 31 had become old for a Colt. Sir Archibald White, who was over 40, could not consider taking up the captaincy again. Yorkshire could look back for inspiration but they had to seek young players, or new players for the future.

1919 was a season of Yorkshire success in an experimental form of the county championship. Matches were confined to two days, but the long playing hours proved unpopular with both public and players and too many matches were too obviously destined to be left drawn. The reckoning was by percentage of matches won in matches played and Yorkshire's final margin of success over Kent was narrow, but as Yorkshire undertook 26 fixtures, winning 12, compared with Kent's 14, giving six victories, general opinion considered Yorkshire to have deserved the honours of the year.

The representative team photograph shows D. C. F. Burton in the captain's place. He came from an East Riding family of cricketing interests and had played in a few county matches before the war. His promise as a batsman was modest but he filled a place in the lower order without appearing to be in the wrong category of cricketer and he had his days of personal delight with 142 not out against Hampshire in 1919 and 110 against Leicestershire in 1921.

In the field Burton was fully qualified at first-class level. Principally in the covers but adaptable anywhere, Burton as Yorkshire's captain could call for fielding excellence by setting an example.

Beside him on the team photograph is E. R. Wilson whose Yorkshire career almost precisely reproduced that of Ernest Smith in another generation. Rockley Wilson, like Ernest Smith, was a schoolmaster who joined the side, mainly in August, as welcome relief and strengthening for the bowling. In age Wilson and Smith were within ten years of each other and both had appeared for Yorkshire before 1900.

Wilson's reappearance in 1919 was therefore a curiosity of cricket. He had not played for the county between 1903 and 1912, he took part in a few matches in 1913 and 1914 and by 1919 he was 40 years old.

Summarising his own career E. R. Wilson said he came back to first-class cricket because he wanted first-hand experience of technical and tactical developments in the game. He must have found some of the principles of his youth still applicable because he enjoyed notable success in his cricketing old age. He took 36 wickets in 1919, 49 in 1920 and 51 in 1921, when he headed the national averages. His bowling was so impressive that he was chosen for the M.C.C. Australian tour of 1920—1.

Ernest Smith was a fast bowler and a hard-hitting tail-end batsman. E. R. Wilson was slow right-arm bowler and a cautious tail-end batsman. Wilson had a rather stumbling approach to the bowling crease and an almost apologetic form of delivery, implying possibility of a leg-break. Possibilities tended to enforce delayed batting decision and when a stroke had to be made it was usually either defensive or desperate. Wilson was a master of accuracy in length. In his best season more than half his overs were maidens.

In the middle row of the 1919 photograph, with Burton and Wilson, sit the senior professionals, Hirst, Rhodes and Denton, already legendary in their playing lifetimes. George Hirst's hair shows white below his cap and under his cap there is no hair of any colour. Rhodes sits erect and by keeping his moustache he ranks himself with the middle-aged of the period. Denton's face carries deep lines. Hirst is 47, Rhodes, 41, Denton 45.

Hirst and Denton are close to the end of their county careers. Rhodes is just beginning another one.

George Hirst bowled fewer than 200 overs in 1919 and took only 18 wickets, but he scored 1,441 runs in all matches, averaging 38.94. He began in wonderful form with a match-saving 180 not out against M.C.C., 80 against Cambridge University, 120 against Essex, 120 against Warwickshire and 88 against the Australian Imperial Forces, all within the first month of the season.

Denton also made his 1,000 runs in spite of a fortnight's absence from the field because of a thumb injury incurred during the Whitsuntide match at Old Trafford where Lancashire won a precious victory mainly through the batting of Makepeace, who was a Yorkshireman by birth, and the bowling of Parkin, who had played for Yorkshire only to be discarded on discovery that he was not a Yorkshireman born, by the width of the River Tees.

Rhodes came back to first-class cricket after alarming reports of league temptation to resume his 1914 place as an opening batsman and to discover that Yorkshire were short of first-class bowling. He scored 1,237 runs and took 164 wickets.

He became, as he had become 20 years earlier, the outstanding slow left-arm bowler in the world. He was, to superficial observation, precisely the bowler of his youth, with the same walking steps into the delivery stride, the same persistence, the same self-confidence in success.

Rhodes himself knew that he was not the same bowler. He knew that he was a little less flexible in the back, a little stiffer in the fingers, a little heavier in the feet. He also knew that no batsman remained in cricket to distinguish between old Rhodes and new Rhodes and that new Rhodes had all the assets necessary for conquest of a new generation of batsmen.

The ball turned less dramatically, but it still turned visibly and could find the bat's edge if not the shoulder. Length asked awkward questions—forward stroke or back? Direction commanded some sort of batting response. Flight acted as a soporific, like the hypnotist's watch swinging before the eyes. The bowling of the first Rhodes pressed batsmen to destruction; the bowling of the second Rhodes lured them.

Rhodes always professed to enjoy batting more than bowling but in 1919 and the seasons immediately following Yorkshire needed Rhodes the bowler even more than they needed Rhodes the batsman. Rhodes bowled—and bowled himself to the head of the averages for five successive seasons, rating E. R. Wilson as only a part-timer in 1921.

No doubt he would have continued as a first-class batsman had necessity demanded. He opened the innings in the early matches of 1919 with the alert, lantern-jawed Percy Holmes who had been feeling his way into the side in 1913 and 1914.

Holmes had obvious talent and was soon among the centuries. So had a younger batsman, who had applied for early demobilisation from the Army to seek a cricket career. His name was Herbert Sutcliffe.

Sutcliffe played his first match for Yorkshire at Gloucester and went to the crease when the fourth wicket fell, George Hirst waiting for him. The wily Dipper was bowling and pitching persistently wide, inviting a stroke of inexperience. After an over or two Sutcliffe heard Hirst say to the bowler: 'It's the lad's first match, why don't you give him a chance to make a shot, if he can?'

A few matches later Sutcliffe did not overhear another suggestion made by George Hirst. It was to the Yorkshire captain, recommending experiment with Holmes and Sutcliffe as partners to open the innings. Their first essay produced 0; by the end of the season they had shared five century stands, including 279 against Northamptonshire and 253 against Lancashire. Yorkshire had settled one of their problems for a generation.

Opening bowlers presented another problem for which solution was not found until halfway through the season. W. E. Blackburne and A. C. Williams had been tried, both enjoying one particularly successful match without promising to fulfil all requirements. Blackburne gave way to Emmott Robinson, who at 35 years of age was an experienced league cricketer with all-round ability. Robinson held his place without achieving any startling performances, but in early July dramatic reinforcement to the bowling came from Abram Waddington of the Laisterdyke club in Bradford.

Waddington's pace was a lively fast-medium, deriving from an action so smooth and flowing that it drew admiring comment wherever he bowled. He was left-handed—though right-handed in batting—with the inherent virtues of his kind and in 19 appearances before the end of the season he had taken 100 wickets.

Regularly in the side, required more for batting than for bowling, was Roy Kilner, who had established his position in 1913 and 1914 and returned to cricket with a war-wound but without disturbance to a cheerful philosophy. Roy and his younger brother Norman had family association with Yorkshire cricket, for they were nephews of Irving Washington. Like his uncle, Roy was a left-hander with an enterprising outlook on batsmanship. Division of interests probably prevented Roy Kilner from reaching the highest levels as either batsman or bowler, but when his career came to untimely end he had scored 13,014 runs and taken 858 wickets for Yorkshire, played for England at home and in Australia and created for himself a cricketing character to be remembered with affection.

Norman Kilner, who was a right-hander, stayed on the edge of the Yorkshire side for five seasons, but no regular place could be found for him and he qualified for Warwickshire where his batting developed a valuable consistency.

Arthur Dolphin was 32 years old when he returned to wicketkeeping for Yorkshire. He played for eight more seasons, to win the highest compliment open to specialists; he was praised by other wicketkeepers, who rated him quickest of all his contemporaries in stumping.

11

Astonishing achievement

In 1920 and 1921 Yorkshire were completing the reorganisaion of their forces. Hirst, appointed coach at Eton, played only in the school holidays and in 1921 came to his formal retirement from first-class cricket. Denton left the side in 1920, taking his customary 1,000 runs from his last season and playing an innings of 209 not out against Worcestershire as rebuttal to increasingly poor health. 1921 was D. C. F. Burton's last year of captaincy and would, by general consent, have been a Yorkshire championship year had rain and sun spread influence more evenly across the counties. Burton's successor was Geoffrey Wilson, whose batting was scarcely equal to county demands but whose tactical functions in the field could be carefully protected by the experienced players.

Consolidation of the side into an immensely powerful unit was contrived without fast bowling but with compensating qualities raised to a high level. G. G. Macaulay was introduced to serve as a fast bowler, but his pace, even from a notably long run-up, was inadequate and he was advised (by George Hirst, of course) to become a medium-pace bowler concentrating on accuracy and off-spin.

Emmott Robinson therefore grew in significance as a new-ball bowler of outswing, opening the attack with the exuberant Waddington. Rhodes remained master of the slow-bowling world, with Kilner complementary rather than competitive. Often enough Rhodes and Kilner bowled in partnership, Rhodes in the classical manner, Kilner, his action characterised by a pronounced flourish of the wrist, going over the wicket to provide a contrast of line for the batsmen.

The vacancy left by Denton at No. 3 in the batting order was occupied by Edgar Oldroyd, who took long-awaited opportunity to translate promise into impressive performance. Oldroyd contributed little to the gaiety of Yorkshire's batting. Infinite patience and the soundest of methods provided him with a rare defensive skill that sometimes came to be exploited for its own sake and was, no doubt, sometimes extended merely as stubborn reaction to protest. On the difficult pitch Oldroyd was an artist; in easier conditions he often seemed content to be a labourer.

When the individual talents were adapted and fitted together, given the fuel of ambition and the lubricating oil of experience, Yorkshire became a conquering team. They won the championship in every season from 1922 to 1925 and in the four years they were defeated only six times in 122 engagements.

Half their victories were completed with an innings to spare, others by enormous margins, and never throughout the period were Yorkshire beaten twice by the same side in one season. The feature of their cricket attracting public attention was not, however, the overwhelming successes but astonishing results achieved against all the probabilities of cricket.

Yorkshire and five or six other counties were expected to dominate the championship. Playing strength and financial resources were unevenly distributed and wide margins separated the leaders and the laggards, but weather is frequently a levelling factor in English cricket and to win where no road to victory seemed open became a Yorkshire characteristic.

In 1922 a rain-interrupted match at Hull was completed for an aggregate of 240 runs. Batting second and scoring 125 Yorkshire were left with a first-innings lead of 30 and little time in hand. They needed only 15 overs. Waddington bowled seven of them to take seven wickets for six runs and Sussex were all out for 20.

In the return match at Hove, Yorkshire, batting first, were put out for 42 by Tate and Roberts. Recovery was comprehensive. Sussex were dismissed for 95, Yorkshire ran up a second-innings total of 228 and the match was finished off with a bowling return of six for 13 by Rhodes in a Sussex score of 83 all out.

In 1928 Surrey took tea on the third day at Sheffield needing

57 to win with seven wickets standing. They were beaten by 25 runs, Kilner taking five evening wickets for a concession of two runs in his complete figures of six for 22.

The Essex match at Leyton was not even within sight of a first-innings decision on the third morning after second-day downpour and when that issue was eventually resolved Yorkshire were 99 runs behind. They won. On the afternoon 'sticky wicket' Rhodes bowled seven overs for five wickets at a cost of eight runs and Yorkshire hurried to 164 for three and astonishing victory.

In 1925 at Bradford Sussex wanted 40 runs to win and had six wickets in hand at lunchtime on the third day. Macaulay took five of those six wickets in six overs and Yorkshire won by 23 runs. Fact would have been discredited had it been presented as fiction.

Of the four successive years of championship success 1923 and 1925 were the most impressive in terms of results. In 1923 there were 25 outright victories in a programme of 31 matches; in 1925 victory came 21 times in 32 matches. 1923 brought one defeat, 1925 none.

With the one dramatic exception, which was, of course, the sensation of the county season, Yorkshire knew virtually uninterrupted triumph through 1923. They won five of the first seven matches, rain compelling two drawn games. They lost to Nottinghamshire, by three runs, and then won 13 matches in succession to make the championship a one-horse race.

Many opponents were simply swept aside. Middlesex at Bradford fielded through a Yorkshire innings of 411 for nine, declared, and were then dismissed for 122 and 60. Rhodes made a century and took five wickets for 29 runs. He did not bowl in the follow-on; Kilner took six for 14.

Northamptonshire at Bradford could not carry the match beyond the second day in fine weather. With totals of 78 and 79 they lost by an innings and 155 runs. Loss of a day's play at Sheffield could not save Gloucestershire from defeat by 10 wickets after Yorkshire had made a declaration at 280 for three. Loss of a day's play could not save Worcestershire at

Harrogate, where totals of 42 and 163 were offered against Yorkshire's 242 for two, declared.

In the August southern tour Yorkshire found a softened pitch at Portsmouth and permitted Hampshire totals of no more than 66 and 52, Macaulay taking five wickets in one innings and six in the other.

More precious than victories over counties whom they were expected to beat easily was the success over Lancashire in the August Bank Holiday fixture. The Bradford ground could not accommodate the crowds; 23,000 people attended on the Saturday and an estimated 26,000 were crammed in on the Monday, with thousands locked out and thousands more turned back as they sought transport from the city.

Lancashire batted first, cautiously and with no more success than a total of 188. It was not big enough for first-innings advantage but R. Tyldesley's patient and accurate bowling kept the Yorkshire lead down to 25 on the second afternoon; one side or the other had to find decisive inspiration. Macaulay took four wickets, Kilner three, E. R. Wilson two and Robinson one, and by close of play Lancashire were all out for 73.

The one Yorkshire failure of the year was essentially a tail-end batting failure at Headingley in early June. Nottinghamshire had gained a first-innings lead of 66 but had dissipated advantage in second-innings batting that produced a total of no more than 95. Rhodes, with six for 23, seemed to have turned the match. Yorkshire must certainly have thought so when they reached a position of needing 36 to win with five wickets standing, but S. J. Staples came suddenly to bowling authority. Macaulay held on grimly for 17 not out, but Robinson, Wilson, Waddington and Dolphin produced one run between them and when Staples took his fifth wicket of the innings Nottinghamshire had won by three runs.

The single lapse emphasised the general strength. Yorkshire rarely needed significant service from tail-end batsmen, Holmes, Sutcliffe, Oldroyd, Kilner, Rhodes and the newly capped Leyland all scored more than 1,000 championship runs. Tailenders were not often given chance of a second innings; Dolphin batted 27 times in 31 matches, Macaulay 29 times in

31 matches, and even Robinson, the usual No. 7, played only 37 championship innings though he took part in all 32 fixtures.

Holmes and Sutcliffe established an astonishing consistency in their opening partnerships. Within a few seasons of being sent in first together they had linked their names in cricket history by setting up new county records and before they were parted by the retirement of Holmes in 1933 they had a world record of 555 to their names and 69 century stands for Yorkshire alone.

Holmes and Sutcliffe opening an innings together were a reassurance to all Yorkshiremen. They came briskly from the pavilion, Holmes usually wearing a cap and often only the right-hand batting glove. Sutcliffe rarely wore a cap and he brushed his hair to shining smoothness. Their preliminaries to taking strike were confident and businesslike, implying long tenancy. Assurance marked their lively running between the wickets and the respect of each for the ability of the other made 'farming' of the bowling unnecessary. Neither had a recognised technical weakness or expressed dislike of any particular bowler or type of bowling. Sutcliffe's imperturbability balanced a suggestion of restlessness in Holmes.

Holmes tended to lead the scoring but always seemed slightly the more vulnerable as indeed the figures prove him to have been, but in the first years of their association they marched almost precisely in step. In the four championship programmes from 1922 to 1925 Holmes played an innings of 50 or more 43 times, Sutcliffe 46 times. Together they raised the 100 on 17 occasions.

In one notable instance they were kept apart by mischance. In 1925 the Middlesex fixture at Headingley was Roy Kilner's benefit match and in the assembling crowds Holmes was delayed on his way to the ground. When Yorkshire won the toss Sutcliffe and Leyland opened the innings and put on 218. Holmes came in at No. 4; Sutcliffe was waiting and this time a third-wicket century partnership was recorded.

Holmes in 1925 was in his finest form. In all matches he scored 2,453 runs and at Lord's he played an innings of 315 not out. Sutcliffe left him when the total was 140—not by dismissal but because of injury—and Holmes stayed through six partnerships until Yorkshire declared at 538.

Holmes's innings was not only huge; it was brilliant. Cutting, hooking and driving with dancer's footwork he hit 38 boundaries and scored at an average rate of more than 50 runs an hour.

Holmes and Sutcliffe never were slow scorers in their major partnerships. Because they proceeded undramatically and with an appearance of inevitability their rate of progress tended to pass unremarked, but investigation into times would suggest that they were in exceptional restraint if they were not collecting 60 or 70 runs an hour.

The achievements of Holmes and Sutcliffe tended to create patterns for the remainder of Yorkshire's batting. When the openers succeeded scope was provided for the accumulation of crushing totals; after the early fall of a wicket efforts were concentrated on making sure of a recovery. Yorkshire's batting was invariably undertaken with the needs of Yorkshire's bowling in mind. The bowlers won the matches; the business of batting was to provide margins of runs and time for the bowlers.

An ideal middle batsman would therefore be one who could force the pace in easy circumstances or 'graft'—to use a term that came later into cricket idiom—when the pitch was difficult or recovery had to be made.

So sure were Yorkshire of a batting discovery in this mould that they gave a cap to Maurice Leyland before he had played 50 innings for the county. The judgement was impeccable. Leyland scored 1,000 runs in his first full season of 1923 and never afterwards failed to score 1,000 runs until the season of his retirement:

12

Not to everybody's liking

During their years at the top of the championship table Yorkshire discovered, or rediscovered, the truth that prolonged success brings problems as well as satisfactions. When victory has become a routine experience threat of defeat assumes a disproportionate anxiety. Failure or disadvantage hurts more deeply. There is danger of record being ranked before reputation.

After the splendours of 1923 Yorkshire found themselves moving towards isolation among the cricket community during 1924. They were accused of unbecoming and unacceptable behaviour.

Beyond all doubt the Yorkshire team had acquired a forceful character. It was illustrated in the manner of some of their cricket and it was contributory to some of their achievements. Without explosiveness in bowlers incredible feats would not have been accomplished. When, as was bound to happen sooner or later, miracles could not be worked frustrations inevitably arose and were not to be accepted philosophically. In short, Yorkshire forgot their sportsmanship.

Success on the field tends to induce support verging on the fanatical. Yorkshire cricket spectators had, like the players, become so accustomed to superiority that anything less was looked upon as a form of injustice. Myopia developed round the boundary edge to such an extent that virtues could be seen only in one team.

When Yorkshire went to Lord's at the end of May in 1924 they had not suffered a championship defeat for a year. The fixture with Middlesex coincided with a Test trial match which took away Holmes, Sutcliffe, Kilner and Macaulay from one county and Hearne and Hendren from the other, and Middlesex, with a predominantly amateur eleven, proved to have much the stronger reserves. Yorkshire batted indifferently in both innings and bowled with so little success that Middlesex were able to declare at 465 for eight and win by an innings.

The humiliation rankled and the return match, at Sheffield in early July, began and ended in a miserable atmosphere of ill-will. Again Yorkshire were not the all-conquering cricketers of their own desire and the crowd's expectation. They won the toss and put Middlesex in first, but the soft pitch was not treacherous and Middlesex scored 358. Spectators expressed their disappointment, loudly and rudely, but their condemnation was not directed towards any shortcomings in their own darlings so much as towards visiting players and the umpires.

Exasperated bowlers could not keep their tongues still and made an ally of the more moronic spectators with a succession of provocative appeals. The match grew more unpleasant as it progressed towards a drawn ending and Middlesex left Sheffield resolved to take the drastic step of declining fixtures with Yorkshire for the following season.

The sorely tried umpires, H. Butt and W. Reeves, made a report naming Waddington as an offender and the Yorkshire committee felt obliged to ask the M.C.C. Cricket Committee to make a full enquiry into allegations.

The report on the enquiry was made public. It supported the umpires and suggested that Waddington should be required to keep his feelings under control on the field, which was, in effect, no compliment to Yorkshire's general behaviour and the authority of the captain.

Details of subsequent negotiations between the committees of Yorkshire and Middlesex were not revealed for public edification, but the outcome of protracted talks and correspondence with a continuation of fixtures.

Under this cloudy sky of controversy Yorkshire approached danger of becoming social outcasts in cricket. Nobody could deny their playing ability but appreciation for their outlook and cricketing manners could be withheld and current opinion was undoubtedly anti-Yorkshire.

Newspaper revelations suggested differences of opinion between Surrey and Yorkshire, and the Oval match, which Surrey won, was made a focus for inflammatory prose, but in this instance no formal communications passed between the county authorities and at the end of the season Yorkshire were left to make their own examination of affairs that had left them unpopular

They came to 1925 with A. W. Lupton as captain and a plain warning from the President, Lord Hawke, that individual international honours were not awarded on cricketing form alone. Lupton was an experienced club cricketer but to enter the first-class ranks at the age of 46 was a severe trial for batting and fielding ability and Lupton wisely limited his personal playing ambitions to concentrate his attention on duties of discipline. His players accepted his function, managing the technical side of the cricket with professional expertise and following the captain's lead in tactful public relations.

Yorkshire kept the championship and won back community respect. They were so clearly the strongest side of the year that they completed their programme without losing a match and held the title by a wide margin.

Macaulay was the bowler of the year and Holmes the batsman. In all matches Macaulay took 211 wickets and confirmed his position among the leading medium-pace off-break bowlers in cricket history. Whenever the pitch helped he turned the ball sharply, he maintained remarkable control of length and direction and his hostility of approach was obvious and unceasing. Batsmen, in Macaulay's view, were permitted to the crease only for the purpose of being dismissed—by Macaulay, for preference. He grudged them every run and particular antagonism was reserved for those who sought quick singles from playing the ball in the vicinity of the bowler.

The passion in Macaulay's bowling supplied the fuel for his most dramatic performances and gave him a strength to endure when a rather frail physique was obviously hard-pressed. Naturally, he preferred the turning pitch and he was luridly uncomplimentary towards groundsmen who were able to prepare a batsman's delight. When conditions were helpful to him he rarely failed to exert his authority and the sight of left-handers at the crease made his eyes gleam as he took his rather long run-up with short strides that made his shoulders sway until he reached the balance of a high delivery.

During a match at Hull when play was held up as the turf was recovering after rain Macaulay was observed pacing impatiently up and down outside the dressing-room.

'What's the matter, Mac?' he was asked. 'Matter?' retorted Macaulay. 'Matter? They have seven left-handers in the side and we can't get on the field.'

In his outstanding season in 1925 Macaulay must have cared little which way round the batsmen stood. He took five wickets in an innings no fewer than 15 times.

Percy Holmes never had a higher season's aggregate than in 1925 when he scored, in all matches, 2,453 runs with an average of 57. From first to last, though the summer was not notable for fine weather, he was in remarkable form and the highest innings of his career, the 315 not out at Lord's, was not a peak in isolation so much as the dominating feature in a mountain range of scoring.

Holmes in form was a delightful batsman. He had a bearing of military perkiness, back straight as a ramrod in his brisk walk, bat equally straight in defensive strokes, cuts and hooks played with the precision of drill movements and the follow-through decorated with a little flourish of the bat.

Holmes, like Macaulay but for different reasons, missed international recognition commensurate with his ability. He played for England in the first Test of the 1921 series against Australia but was engulfed in the devastation of fast bowling and was given no further opportunity by panic-stricken selectors.

When Hobbs, who was not available to England in 1921, came into association with Sutcliffe in 1924 all other opening batsmen were reduced to substitutes and England could offer little to such distinguished players as Holmes, Russell and Sandham. Compensation for Holmes was a tour of South Africa in 1927-8 where his Test-match fortune varied from four innings exceeding 50 to conclusion with a 'pair of spectacles'.

This tour provided Holmes and Sutcliffe with their one

opportunity to enjoy a birthday partnership at the crease. On November 25th they made an apppropriate century opening for M.C.C. against Orange Free State. Throughout their playing days Holmes and Sutcliffe believed they had a common anniversary, Holmes the elder by seven years, and they were punctilious in exchanging greetings, but Sutcliffe subsequently discovered that he was a day older than he had thought and a pleasant fiction had to be dispelled by corrections in the later record books.

Percy Holmes never allowed the vicissitudes of his career to depress his spirits. He enjoyed his cricket and the cricketing life of a first-class professional. He fielded as eagerly as he batted and was brilliant in both the outfield and in the slips. The Yorkshire of the 1930s became known as 'the Circus' because of his nonchalant resolution of a travelling difficulty. Arriving late one night at their appointed hotel the players found that a confusion of bookings left them apparently without accommodation. 'The rooms are wanted for Somebody and his Circus,' explained the hotel receptionist. 'Well, they are wanted for Percy Holmes and his Circus,' insisted Holmes, and signed the register to that effect.

13

Decline without collapse

In 1926, as in 1925, Yorkshire were undefeated in championship matches, but they had to hand over the title to Lancashire, who finished first with a tiny advantage in mathematics. There was no manifest injustice in the final placings because Yorkshire finished the season rather weakly whereas Lancashire went from strength to strength and were preparing for a three-year run of success.

Yorkshire's decline was in no sense a collapse. Though five years passed before they won the championship again they were second in the table in two seasons of the period, third twice and their lowest position was fourth. In 142 matches they were defeated only seven times.

Loss of power was in the bowling. Their batting was virtual insurance against outright defeat, but Robinson in his forties was inevitably becoming less effective as a new-ball bowler and Waddington was probably more handicapped than might have appeared after a shoulder injury caused by a fall on slippery turf. 1925 was the last year in which he took 100 wickets and at the end of 1927 he declined the terms offered for continued engagement.

Another accident proved to have delayed consequences. In the Old Trafford match of 1926 a fast bumper from McDonald struck Oldroyd on the head and necessitated hospital attention. Oldroyd was out of cricket for the rest of the season and though he came back in 1927 and made his 1,000 runs for four more years he never seemed to bat with quite the same assurance against the faster bowling and his defensive inclinations grew more pronounced.

In the spring of 1928 the cricket world was shocked by the death at the age of 37 of Roy Kilner. With Leyland he had fulfilled a winter coaching engagement in India and on the homeward journey he became desperately ill with para-typhoid fever. He lived to reach England and be taken from the ship by ambulance to hospital in Barnsley, but he died on April 5th.

His last season of 1927 was not his best but there had been no signs of any significant deterioration in either batting or bowling and he was still clearly among the leading all-rounders in English cricket.

Yorkshire could afford the loss of his batting more than of his bowling. Much of Kilner's bowling service was outside the normal range of the slow left-hander because he was required as a stabiliser, to bowl economically for long spells when slow bowling had little prospect of taking wickets. In these circumstances he approached from over the wicket, concentrating on direction and seeking to induce the mis-hit of impatience rather than despair.

In bowling he could limit himself to the utmost economy but in batting he was inclined to be profligate. He would go to the wicket with the best of intentions to avoid temptations but cheerfulness invariably broke into his philosophy and a-hunting he would go outside the off-stump.

He played his cricket in the best of spirit and his character communicated itself to the crowds, who enjoyed both the earnestness in his bowling and the adventure in his batting. They gave him, in 1925, a benefit of over £4,000 as measure of their high appreciation.

Kilner's death and Waddington's retirement forced Yorkshire into another period of experiment and it was undertaken, in the seasons of 1928 and 1929, under new captaincy. When A. W. Lupton left the office vacant there was no obvious successor at hand and in the autumn of 1927 the committee set aside a tradition of more than 40 years by offering the post to Herbert Sutcliffe without suggesting that he should change his professional status.

Yorkshire have always been considered conservative in their cricketing outlook and Lork Hawke in particular came to be regarded as an apostle of tradition, yet some of the most far-reaching changes in cricket administration and customs were of Yorkshire origin. Yorkshire instituted the system of winter pay. Yorkshire proposed formation of the Board of Control. Yorkshire appointed a professional in a period of amateur captaincy.

Their 1927 decision roused immediate controversy, not only on grounds of its novelty but in the selection of Sutcliffe. Rhodes was still playing. Where diverse opinions were promptly and loudly expressed from many quarters Rhodes characteristically kept his own counsel. Sutcliffe received the committee's letter of invitation in South Africa where he was on tour with M.C.C.

He replied by cable, counting the cost like a true Yorkshireman yet revealing his own clearsightedness and sense of the appropriate.

'Official invitation received yesterday. Many thanks you and committee great honour. Question carefully considered. Regret to decline. Willing to play under any captain elected.'

The captain elected was W. A. Worsley, heir to the baronetcy and estates at Hovingham in the North Riding. W. A. Worsley, later Sir William, was a lifelong cricketing enthusiast who had played in the Eton XI but had never entered the first-class ranks before he took over the Yorkshire captaincy. He enjoyed the experience, the players enjoyed his company and Yorkshire gained a conscientious administrator who subsequently served as their President and as a President of M.C.C.

In the transition from one period of dominance to another Yorkshire were fortunate in maintaining links that prevented them from falling into weakness. Rhodes, Macaulay and Robinson could match the bowling of most counties. Holmes, Sutcliffe, Oldroyd and Leyland provided an enviable batting foundation.

Batting introductions were more immediately successful, probably because they were less speculative. Arthur Mitchell and Wilfred Barber were obviously of first-class quality and needed only opportunity and experience to confirm their claims. Playing 31 innings in 1928 Mitchell scored 1,304 runs and averaged 50. Barber followed Mitchell in long apprenticeship as 12th man, coming to his first Yorkshire century in 1929 and his first 1,000 runs in 1932.

Maurice Leyland had enjoyed a less laborious climb to establishment. His promise as a powerful left-handed batsman was so impressive that he was given his cap after unusually brief experience and he justified the award with 1,000 runs in every season from 1923 to 1939. By 1928 he was playing for England and he was a member of A. P. F. Chapman's team touring Australia in 1928–9.

Leyland was ideally suited to the life of a first-class cricketer. Natural talent gave him the self-confidence to be sure that he could not have been better employed in another career. Membership of a cricketing family gave him a foundation for ready learning from experience. A placid temperament soothed away the minor irritations of play and travel and geniality and genuine appreciation for talent in others brought him universal popularity. He came into county cricket as a skilful and enterprising batsman. He matured into one of the greatest fighting forces Test cricket has ever known.

In their search for new bowling after Waddington's departure and as Rhodes and Robinson approached retirement Yorkshire made many experiments. They encouraged T. A. Jacques, a most impressive fast bowler from York, and would gladly have taken him into the regular ranks, but Jacques found that his legs would not permit full seasons of first-class cricket.

C. H. Hall, F. Dennis and, later, A. C. Rhodes were tried as fast or medium-fast bowlers and a brief look was taken at a leg-break bowler, H. Bedford from Barnsley. The wanted recruits were enlisted during the captaincy of W. A. Worsley in 1928 and 1929. Their names were Bowes and Verity.

14

Rekindling fires

W. E. Bowes, whose early request when publicity beamed on him was 'Call me Bill', came to Yorkshire from the M.C.C. ground staff. He was a Yorkshireman born and was playing club cricket in Leeds when he answered an advertisement for ground staff at Lords.

He was invited for trial and in the cold and darkness of January made his first visit to London and to Lord's. He bowled on a net pitch of matting laid on concrete and the batsmen appointed to investigate possibilities included P. F. Warner and R. Aird, Warner a great figure of M.C.C., Aird then the assistant secretary. Bowes was offered engagement for one season at £5 a week.

Before going to Lord's Bowes had also sent in an application for trial to Warwickshire and Yorkshire's secretary F. C. Toone heard of both approaches. He asked Bowes to see him and recommended an engagement with M.C.C. rather than Warwickshire, suggesting that Bowes would find greater scope at Lord's—and would also be available to Yorkshire from there.

Bowes accepted an M.C.C. engagement, having successfully bargained an additional £1 a week, and never went to Warwickshire for trial. Once before Warwickshire had been in tentative negotiation that came to nothing with a bowler from Yorkshire. His name was Wilfred Rhodes.

In his first season as an M.C.C. professional, in his first match of first-class rating—M.C.C. *v* Cambridge University—Bowes did the hat-trick. The achievement was noted in Yorkshire. In the next season, 1929 he played occasionally and eagerly for the county and took 45 wickets to finish second to Rhodes in the averages.

Yorkshire were not, apparently, entirely convinced and, seeking the best of both worlds, did not dissuade Bowes from signing a nine-year contract which gave M.C.C. first call on his services. On these terms Bowes came to play against his native county on several occasions.

In his second Yorkshire season Bowes was joined in probation by Hedley Verity, whose first season was also no more than half a season. Verity had been seen once or twice in the Yorkshire second team but his early professional career was with Lancashire league clubs, where his slow-medium left-arm bowling was effective and his personal qualities were greatly admired. He came to county cricket with technique already acquired and was so adaptable to the new environment that he took 64 wickets in 407 overs.

Yorkshire could reasonably consider 1930 as their year of change-over. It introduced Verity and confirmed Bowes; it brought the retirement of Rhodes. It left Arthur Wood firmly established as wicket-keeping successor to Arthur Dolphin. It gave sight of the great team to come as the embers of a great team past were being raked out.

The captain for the year was A. T. Barber, an Oxford 'Blue' from a Sheffield family of distinguished cricketers. On appointment, Barber had hoped for more than one season of county cricket, but a scholastic opportunity came his way that compelled resignation from the captaincy at the end of the year. With an average below 20 Barber scarcely did himself justice as a batsman, but he was admirable in the field and his leadership was a happy blend of authority and good humour that made business a pleasure for the whole team.

Good humour was desirable. The summer was wet and frustrating hours had to be spent in the dressing-room. Two matches in succession, at Chesterfield and Harrogate, were abandoned without a ball bowled and of the 28 championship fixtures 15 were left drawn. Yorkshire won 11 games, were beaten twice and came third in the final table.

Wilfred Rhodes did not begin the season with any declared intention of making it his last. He was 52 years old, batting in the lower half of the order and bowling as second and third change, but he could still play an innings of 80 not out and return bowling figures of seven for 35 and four wickets in each innings of a follow-on match.

Decision to leave Yorkshire came with offer of appointment as senior coach at Harrow School. The end of his first-class cricket came at the Scarborough Festival. In his last innings for Yorkshire he scored 41. In his last match, playing for Leveson-Gower's XI against the Australians, he took five wickets and with a livelier fieldsman at mid-off could have had Bradman caught for 0.

To note that Rhodes bowled to Bradman and to Grace is in itself to emphasise the span and the marvel of his career. All added up his runs came to 39,788 and his wickets to 4,184. He scored 1,000 runs and took 100 wickets in 1903 and again in 1926 and in 14 other seasons in between. His first and last Test matches were separated by 20 years. In 1900 he took 261 wickets, in 1901 he took 251 and in 1902 213. He scored over 2,000 runs in the seasons of 1909 and 1911.

Wilfred Rhodes was not a cricketer to catch the popular and ephemeral fancy. His name was not over-publicised in his spells of success and forgotten as quickly as it was illuminated. He was not an innovator. He brought no new technique in bowling, no new stroke into batsmanship.

His bowling was based on the same principles in his first season and his last. Accuracy of length and direction was always the primary consideration. His early spin and his later subtleties of flight made good bowling into great bowling, but the fundamentals were never sacrificed. At all periods of his career he would have offered ideal illustration for an elementary textbook on his craft. He was never less than professionally competent.

His batting methods did change, for reasons of professional competence. To 1914 he was orthodox in the manner of the times, his strokes developing from positions with the left shoulder pointing towards the bowler. After the First World War he adopted a pronounced open stance, that is with the left shoulder pointing towards mid-on or even mid-wicket.

The change brought accusations implying loss of mobility

ABOVE Wilfred Rhodes, all-rounder, going out to bat (left) and bowl (right). Rhodes had the distinction of bowling to both Grace and Bradman

BELOW LEFT G. H. Hirst, who developed the 'George Hirst swerve' and the 'George Hirst pull'

BELOW RIGHT Tom Emmett, of whom W. G. Grace said that on his day he was unplayable

Yorkshire's most famous opening pair, Herbert Sutcliffe and Percy Holmes

Maurice Leyland, the Yorkshire batsman who scored seven centuries for England against Australia

G. G. Macaulay, taken at Scarborough in 1928

A. B. Sellers, a former captain of the county

Sir Leonard Hutton batting during his record score of 364 against Australia

and gracefulness, but critics were inclined to note the surface appearance and overlook the practical applications.

From his open stance Rhodes found he could still move and in his case move more effectively into the orthodox playing positions most frequently required. These were on the back foot because bowling offered less and less encouragement to front-foot play. In his own batting and in his coaching Rhodes became an advocate of the back foot. It was a policy of realism, ultimately reflected in the achievements of an Australian named Bradman.

Though Rhodes never roused the cricket following to ecstasies he always commanded admiration for his accomplishment, for his dignity and for his integrity. With the lengthening of his career admiration was augmented by immense respect and increasing wonder. He became not so much a favourite in cricket as a pride of cricket. His walk to the wicket or the removal of his sweater before a bowling spell brought the same recognition that greets the appearance of a distinguished conductor in the preliminaries of an orchestral concert. He had no need to prove himself further; honour was already earned.

All Yorkshire cricket, all the world's cricket, was indebted to Rhodes, but the extent was not public knowledge. Rhodes could sometimes be seen as managing director of Yorkshire in the field, but the indirect influence of Rhodes and Emmott Robinson could be measured only as the recipients came to reveal their benefit.

Bowes and Verity have been wholehearted in expression of their gratitude. They learned by discourse in which events of the day's play came under analysis. Verity was told that his seven wickets for 26 should have been seven for 22 because an unnecessary boundary had been conceded. Bowes was informed of the difference between bowling to take wickets without consideration of cost and bowling with economy in mind.

Education, of course, involves two parties; the teacher and the taught. Bowes and Verity would, no doubt, have come to bowling greatness had they never played in Yorkshire teams with Rhodes and Robinson, but time would have been wasted. Rhodes and Robinson would have left a smaller cricketing legacy had Bowes and Verity been less receptive to tuition and less skilled in application. They learned gratefully, they learned quickly and Rhodes and Robinson left in their hands the striking weapons for another period of championship triumph.

It began in 1931.

15

Design of dedication

Yorkshire were captained in 1931 by F. E. Greenwood, who had played some useful innings for the county in 1930 and who was as enterprising in the field as he tried to be at the crease. He led Yorkshire optimistically and he led them, ironically, through a season without defeat except for one match which made history in captaincy.

The 1931 summer was wet, particularly in May and early June, and when the second day of the match against Gloucestershire at Sheffield was abandoned Yorkshire had endured their fourth successive experience of 'No Play Today'. In mutual evening commiseration the captains, Greenwood and B. H. Lyon, turned their ingenuity towards defiance of the weather and concocted a scheme that made the controversy of the season and led eventually to revision of rules.

In the championship system of the year an outright victory was worth 15 points and in a drawn match eight points were shared, equally if there were no first innings result but with five for the winners and three for the losers if a first-innings decision could be reached.

Given only the last day for play, Greenwood and Lyon—or more probably, Lyon and Greenwood—concocted a device to make the full 15 points available from their match.

No public announcement of overnight deliberations was made before the start of play. Yorkshire won the toss and gave Gloucestershire first innings. Dipper and Sinfield went to the wicket and Emmott Robinson bowled the first ball, which went to the boundary for byes. The players made their way back to the pavilion.

In the press box an exasperated and unenlightened Press Association cricket reporter declared, with embellishment, that it was raining again.

He was wrong; there was no rain, there was more cricket

and there was a full day's work for him. Gloucestershire, by prearranged plan, had declared their innings closed. When Yorkshire batted, represented by Holmes and Wood, the same procedure of concession and declaration was followed, Hammond bowling the one ball to bring the scores to equality.

With first innings thus disposed of as quickly as possible, the points equally shared in case of further rain, Yorkshire and Gloucestershire had the rest of the day to play one innings each with the full 15 championship points at stake.

Gloucestershire won them, scoring 171 to Yorkshire's 124, Verity taking seven wickets and Goddard five at a much cheaper rate. Ingenuity inevitably brought widespread reaction. In some quarters Lyon and Greenwood were praised for bringing life and significance to a dormant cricketing situation. From other quarters the innovating captains were reprimanded for breach of tradition, for circumvention of the law's intent, for opening the way to mockery of championship principles and cricketing practices.

The example was followed on four other occasions during the season—once again by Yorkshire in their match with Northamptonshire at Bradford—but Lord Hawke, as Yorkshire President, spoke against the practice and the counties realised that they had more to lose than gain by any encouragement to flout their own regulations. Rules were revised to make a first-innings declaration illegal without at least an hour's batting.

The 15 points gained by Gloucestershire were not decisive in the final table, for Yorkshire were 66 points ahead of them and were unquestionably the side of the season. Their performances after mid-June were brilliant in the extreme, containing two sequences of five victories in successive matches and one serious threat of defeat.

Three players enjoyed outstanding personal success. Verity took 138 wickets in the championship engagements, Bowes took 109 and Sutcliffe scored 2,049 runs with an average of 97.57.

Here, obviously, lay the foundation of championship success, but the strength was the strength of a dedicated team. Macaulay and Robinson were invaluable in their bowling support. Holmes shared with Sutcliffe six century opening partnerships, including one of 323 against Lancashire and another of 309 against Warwickshire. The authority of their batting was reflected in the rate of scoring: they made 323 in four hours and a half and 309 in three hours and 40 minutes.

Holmes, Mitchell and Leyland showed the variable form that might have been expected from batsmen in a summer of such disturbed weather, but Sutcliffe was astonishingly consistent. In all first-class matches he scored 3,006 runs and averaged 96.96, which was 27 runs an innings more than the second batsman in the national list. In county matches alone the gap between first and second was even wider; Holmes was 38 runs behind.

Sutcliffe knew no week of failure. His first century was 173 not out against Cambridge University in Yorkshire's opening tour and in the closing match of the Scarborough Festival he made 126. He played in two of the three Tests against New Zealand, batted twice and reached his 100 each time. For Yorkshire he made centuries in four successive innings, the third of them raising some comment in Kent.

Sutcliffe had been selected for the Lord's Test, which coincided with Kent's home match with Yorkshire. Sutcliffe withdrew from the Test on the plea of a strained leg muscle but considered himself justified in appearing for his county. Whilst Woolley was scoring 80 for England, Sutcliffe was at Folkestone where he batted for five hours to contribute 230 towards an innings victory for Yorkshire. Kent could only inconvenience Yorkshire; they made them stay overnight and come to the ground for one over to take the last wicket on the third morning.

Sutcliffe's splendour of 1931 formed part of an almost incredible period in his career. From May 1931 to the March ending of the Australia and New Zealand tour of 1932-3—that is two English seasons and one tour—he scored 7,687 runs in 116 innings for an overall average of 79. This performance was the culmination of 12 successive seasons, at home and abroad, in which he never failed to average 50 runs an innings.

Sutcliffe's great authority was long established in 1931. Verity and Bowes were building theirs. Verity reached Test-match status. Bowes confirmed all his early promise and took the step that made him the most effective new-ball bowler of his time. He learned to bowl and control the outswinger.

He became more than a fast bowler. His pace was lively enough and his exceptional height enabled him to pitch a length that could draw an unwilling forward stroke yet lift the ball sharply to shoulder of the bat or to fingers. With swing as well as lift Bowes had too many weapons for most batsmen at county level.

When conditions were discouraging to the more advanced arts Bowes could also bowl bumpers. Here again his height and high action gave him natural advantages. He did not have to pitch crudely short of a length to make the ball lift alarmingly and as a cricketer of intelligence he quickly learned selectivity in his use of the bumper. He used it to startle the wits, not to cause physical injury. Batsmen showing no disturbance of demeanour and who could hook saw little of the Bowes bumper. Nobody knew when it was coming because Bowes had an ambling run-up that gave a false impression of the effort instilled into the delivery itself. Bowes had a giant's strength but he knew better than to dissipate it to no purpose and Yorkshire helped to conserve it.

Bowes was expected to hold the catches that came his way at mid-on but he was positively forbidden to exhaust himself in ground fielding. When he was bowling everything possible was done to ensure that the ball was returned easily to him and the shine on the new ball was so precious that elaborate precautions were taken to preserve it.

As a batsman Bowes received no encouragement whatever. Where the young Rhodes was told, 'Now, Wilfred, not more than 20,' Bowes was not even allowed to go to the crease if his innings could reasonably be eliminated. In 25 championship matches of 1931 Bowes had 11 innings.

The fielding co-operation provided for Bowes was also applied to Verity, whose left-arm bowling, nearer to medium pace than to slow, was given creative assistance that originated new standards in field-setting. Verity was not as tall as Bowes but he was near six feet and his action was classically high.

With these advantages he could make the turning ball lift unusually high on the bat and even the defensive strokes with a 'dead' bat offered catching opportunities. Yorkshire took them by stationing fieldsmen a yard or two closer than customary in the normal positions of gully, short leg, silly mid-off and silly mid-on.

The fieldsmen were obviously taking risks, of which no one was more conscious than the bowler. For safety's sake alone Verity had to be meticuluous in accuracy; one untimely long hop of full toss could be cause of a serious injury. Gratitude for fielding enterprise that brought sensational bowling analyses could be best expressed by eliminating errors of length and direction.

Verity bowled with remarkable control and Yorkshire fielded with remarkable nerve and anticipation. Emmott Robinson at silly mid-off, Macaulay on the on side and Mitchell in the gully became as characteristic a feature of Yorkshire cricket as Holmes and Sutcliffe opening the innings.

Verity also had the invaluable asset of being a lucky cricketer. Rhodes and Hirst bowled all their lives without ever taking all 10 wickets in an innings. Verity won the distinction in his first full season and twice in his career.

His 1931 performance was at Headingley against Warwickshire. It was Yorkshire's first home match of the season and was proceeding along prosaic lines before it came to a startling end. Warwickshire, having won the toss, made 201 and were 97 behind on first innings after Holmes and Sutcliffe had founded the Yorkshire total on a partnership of 120.

Verity began and ended his second-innings bowling on the second evening. The pitch gave him no exceptional help. He simply bowled at the top of his form, catches went to hand and were held, Mitchell taking three in the gully.

The second time Verity took all 10 wickets in an innings was in the next season, 1932. Again the match was at Headingley, but on this occasion, with Nottinghamshire the opponents, the game went into the third day. Yorkshire stood at 163 for nine against Nottinghamshire's 234 when a thunderstorm ended play on the second day and after a delayed resumption on the last morning Nottinghamshire were 38 for no wicket at lunch.

They were all out for 67. In 20 overs, of which 16 were maidens, Verity took 10 wickets for 10 runs. The colloquialism of paralysed batsmen took on literal application.

With 139 runs wanted for victory Holmes and Sutcliffe required no assistance. On a drying pitch, after having watched six batsmen fail to score in a fantastic collapse, they hit off the runs in 90 minutes.

16

Principles and principals

In his presidential review of 1931 Lord Hawke offered comforting prophecy for 1932 and beyond and won honour in his own county. Yorkshire kept the championship.

They kept it by exercise of the same cricketing principles and mainly through the performances of the same principals. In 1932 Sutcliffe scored 2,883 runs for Yorkshire and 3,336 in all; Bowes and Verity between them took 314 wickets for Yorkshire.

Some replacements were required in the side. Oldroyd and Robinson had retired and Greenwood, though re-elected captain, was able to play in only seven matches because of family business obligations.

Oldroyd's departure made room for the waiting Wilfred Barber, who established himself with 1,000 runs in polished manner and with impressive fielding, mainly on the boundary edge. As a new-ball bowler A. C. Rhodes played in most of the matches to take 40 wickets and T. F. Smailes and C. H. Hall were brought in occasionally as fast-medium bowlers.

In Greenwood's absence the captaincy was undertaken by A. B. Sellers, elder son of Arthur Sellers who had played for Yorkshire at the turn of the century and was elected a vice-president in 1931. Brian Sellers learned his cricket at St. Peter's school, York, and in the Bradford league and he came to the county side as a batsman of determination, a fieldsman of inexhaustible energy and a captain of passionate devotion to duty.

In the arts of both playing and captaincy he came as a learner, but no sooner was he in full authority than he began to show an impressive personality that made him a contributor to the character of Yorkshire cricket.

Brian Sellers remained a batsman of modest attainment,

by his own assessment at least. He always maintained that he could never have been considered for the England captaincy simply because he was not a good enough player, but at county level he made experience and resolution serve as substitute for any lack of native ability and he left examples of commendable performance in the records. He made centuries against the Australians, Cambridge University, Kent and Nottinghamshire and he exceeded 1,000 runs in the season of 1938. He was certainly not a negligible factor in the Yorkshire batting strength and though limitations of footwork left him vulnerable to spin he was unflinching against fast bowling.

The aspect of courage in his character gave him the desired and admired qualities of leadership. He was an inspiration through the longest day in the field. In the covers he was untiring and he developed a notable capacity to pick up and throw powerfully on the turn, sometimes with both feet off the ground. In the close positions of gully, silly mid-off or on the leg side he was always prepared to be a leader, never asking his players to take risks he was not prepared to accept for himself.

He was essentially of the team as distinct from being with the team. Their interests and their welfare were his and however scathing he might have had to be in private dressing-room discipline his public identification was always with his players. He represented them loyally in committee and he was their advocate in all matters beneficial to their comfort and efficiency.

On his recommendation a full-time professional masseur travelled with the side throughout the summer, the first appointment being given to B. Heyhirst, who became a Yorkshire cricket character in his own right, and, predictably, a devoted servant of A. B. Sellers.

As the players came to appreciate the dedication of Sellers and to recognise his integrity a strong sense of self-discipline grew into the side. Dressing-room customs for mutual advantage were adopted. A social as well as a cricketing unity was established.

Sellers was, of course, fortunate in his time. He could not have been so outstandingly successful in county captaincy without the material of a team that could scarcely have failed to be successful without any captain at all.

1932, the year of Sellers' acting captaincy, illustrated the Yorkshire capacity. Two matches were lost and two completely abandoned in the wet weather of May and early June, yet the championship was won by a wide margin. From their last 15 fixtures Yorkshire took 14 victories.

In their performances astonishment piled on astonishment. At Leyton Holmes and Sutcliffe set up a world record first-wicket partnership. At Bradford the match with Gloucestershire burst at the seams with memorable cricket. Against Nottinghamshire Verity returned his bowling figures of 10 wickets for 10 runs. The defeat of Essex at Scarborough contained cricket beyond all rationality. In nine innings Yorkshire raised totals of over 400; opponents were dismissed for less than 100 ten times. Ten matches were won with an innings to spare—and one lost by such margin.

The innings defeat was bitter, because it was before a Yorkshire crowd at Bradford and because it was inflicted by Lancashire. The start of the game was delayed and the pitch was always soft, but Lancashire took charge and never let go. Paynter created their advantage with such devastating hitting that he scored 50 runs in half an hour and went on to make 152 in three hours and a half. Verity's eight wickets were a reasonable expectation, but not at a cost of 107 runs.

Wickets for Lancashire's Frank Sibbles were also a reasonable expectation, but not at a rate of seven for 10 runs. Yorkshire were all out for 46, of which Sutcliffe made 27, and following-on were all out again for 167—of which Sutcliffe made 61.

In the Yorkshire season Sutcliffe made 12 centuries with 313 at Leyton as his highest score. It would have been 314, at least, if he could have gazed into a crystal ball instead of at a cricket ball.

The match against Essex was not regarded of any special significance when Holmes and Sutcliffe opened the Yorkshire innings on the first morning. Sutcliffe was in customary self-assurance but Holmes was experiencing some stiffness in the back and would not have been dismayed had an early chance to the wicketkeeper been taken.

It was missed and no further opportunity came to Essex all day. Yorkshire's score at the close was 423 for no wicket.

A record in sight drew public attention. Holmes and Sutcliffe had to push their way into the Leyton ground on the second morning and the dressing-room was littered with messages of congratulations, good wishes and adjuration. One Yorkshire enthusiast had made an overnight journey from Hull.

Yorkshire's players were as anxious as anyone that a new record should be attempted and created, but in the accepted outlook records were incidental to the course of the match and Yorkshire wanted to be fielding after lunch. Spectators had come in thousands to see Holmes and Sutcliffe extend a partnership, but Yorkshire had come to Leyton to win a match.

Re-starting was harder than starting for the batsmen. They suffered inescapable physical reaction from their first-day exertion. They were conscious of abnormal tension. With another 132 runs to be made prolonged concentration was required. Each batsman had to be as concerned for the other as for himself. More than the mechanics of batting was demanded.

The runs were made. At what cost in self-discipline and weariness of the flesh only Holmes and Sutcliffe could say, but after the scoreboard had turned to 555 Herbert Sutcliffe the imperturbable hit wildly at the next ball and played on.

With 40 minutes remaining before lunch declaration would in any event have been made at the end of the over, but as the players walked away to acclamation a horror of uncertainty developed. The scoreboard turned back to 554; the scorebooks did not tally.

Press pandemonium was created. Messages and corrections flashed across the cables of the world. A painful scrutiny of scorebook detail had to be undertaken and comparison revealed the difference of one run, attributable to a no-ball unrecorded in one book. The new record was established.

This was almost the last great partnership between Holmes and Sutcliffe. Later in 1932 Holmes had to miss matches because of an injured knee and though he underwent an operation after the season ended he was never at his best in 1933.

Sutcliffe continued to stride along a pathway of personal success. He went from Leyton to a Test trial at Old Trafford where he scored 96 and 110 not out and rejoined Yorkshire to play an innings of 270 against Sussex.

In July Yorkshire met Gloucestershire at Bradford. Holmes and Sutcliffe began the match with a century partnership, but the sparkle in Yorkshire's total of 472 for seven wickets was provided by Mitchell, whose 177 not out was scored in three hours and 40 minutes.

Gloucestershire were also in batting form and enterprising mood. Sinfield making 110 and Dacre 71, only to be obscured by Hammond who batted for two hours and 10 minutes to score 147, with six sixes and 18 fours.

After all this ready scoring Yorkshire still thought of an outright victory—for Yorkshire, of course. They needed a big lead and a few hours of time on the wearing pitch of the third day. They built the lead by scoring 240 for six wickets in two hours, Sutcliffe hitting six sixes and eight fours in an innings of 132 that completed his century of centuries in first-class cricket. The last Gloucestershire wicket was taken when 'last over' had been called.

Reaction to more prosaic achievement never set in. Yorkshire went on winning and winning in wondrous ways. Verity took his 10 for 10, Lancashire paid for Whitsuntide victory with August Bank Holiday defeat and at Scarborough Essex met Sutcliffe again.

They came with businesslike intent, represented by a stronger side than at Leyton and including a young fast bowler named Kenneth Farnes. The weather was exceptionally hot and the pitch was fast and true. Essex were glad to win the toss.

Their first innings occupied most of the first day and brought a total of 325. It was essentially a battle between the batsmen and Bowes because only fast bowling could be expected to induce batting mistakes. Bowes answered the call with 41 overs, taking nine wickets for 121 runs. He tired himself to utter exhaustion and a night of sleeplessness through cramp.

In the late evening Yorkshire avoided the possibility of accident to their leading batsmen and Sutcliffe went in at No. 4 on the second morning. His first partnership was with Mitchell, who gave dutiful support as Sutcliffe swept a majestic way to a century in less than two hours. His second partnership was with Leyland, whose arrival prompted Essex to make a desperate assault with their young fast bowler.

Farnes bowled with all the speed he could command and when he found himself being driven he pitched short. In 55 minutes Sutcliffe and Leyland put on 149 runs, six successive overs providing 102 of them. Sutcliffe advanced his personal score from 100 to 194 in 40 minutes.

From declaration at 476 for nine wickets—Bowes excused from batting exertion—Yorkshire proceeded quietly to another innings victory.

The outstanding successes of Sutcliffe, Bowes and Verity inevitably shadowed other individual performances of the 1932 season, but the supporting play carried distinction in its own right. Macaulay remained among the most accurate bowlers in cricket and Leyland enjoyed an August that brought him more than 1,000 of his 1,821 runs. With Barber he set up a Yorkshire record of 343 for the second wicket and so wrote his name in three wicket-partnership records for the county. In 1928 he had made 323 with Sutcliffe for the third wicket and in 1926 he had shared 276 with Emmott Robinson for the sixth.

Among Yorkshire's supplementary bowlers of 1932 was Horace Fisher, a slow-medium left-hander who had first played in 1928 and went on appearing until 1936 without ever meeting all first-class needs. Fisher was a cautious bowler, notably successful in league cricket where he found he could return impressive figures by bowling persistently on a defensive length and waiting for unprofitable batting adventure. First-class batsmen had more time at their disposal and were more adept at accumulation in safe singles. Fisher served a purpose as a relieving bowler but Yorkshire wanted more than that and could not persuade him to widen his outlook.

Fisher did return two spectacular analyses of six for 11 and five for 12 in 1932, the second figures, against Somerset at Sheffield, including a hat-trick in which all three batsmen were l.b.w. When the umpire, W. Reeves, put up his finger for the third time he felt constrained to say, 'As God's my witness, he's out'.

17

On the peaks

Through the decade of the 1930s Yorkshire remained the great force in county cricket. The only seasons they were not champions were 1934 when they gave more than they could afford to England for the Tests against Australia and 1936 when weather and injuries were significant, though not necessarily decisive.

In 1934 England took Leyland and Verity for all five Tests against Australia, Sutcliffe for four and Bowes for three. Sutcliffe would have played throughout the series but for injury and Bowes indicated by taking 19 wickets that the selectors had little justification for leaving him out at Trent Bridge and Old Trafford. When Yorkshire came to review their own season they found that five of their seven defeats were at Test-match times.

By 1936 Macaulay had retired. He ended his cricket career in poor health, troubled with rheumatic onset that permitted him to bowl in no more than 14 innings during his final season of 1935. He was under handicap and in disappointing form through 1934, when he took only 55 wickets in contrast to 1933 when he was a leading bowler with 141 wickets.

In his later seasons Macaulay confined himself almost entirely to off-spin bowling at medium pace, but he never ceased to attack with the spirit and antagonism associated with the character of fast bowling. He bemoaned opportunity denied by perfection of the pitch, but never diminished endeavour. He rejoiced, without dissembling, in the discomfiture of batsmen.

At Old Trafford in 1933 Lancashire had made experiments in pitch preparation and the Whitsuntide match against Yorkshire contained an early prophecy that the game would end on the first day. 'It's like Blackpool sands out there,' said Percy Holmes. A tremendous defensive century by Mitchell, who stayed for six hours on the broken, dusty pitch, falsified the alarming forecasts without upsetting its fundamental logic.

One day's batting was enough for Lancashire. They were dismissed for totals of 93 and 92 and felt no cause for shame. Macaulay took seven wickets in the first innings and five in the second and expressed regret over the end of the match. 'I'm sorry they can't go in again,' he said.

When conditions were helpful to him he rarely missed a bowling opportunity. His length and direction were so notably accurate that a mistake was a surprise to the batsman. 'It's a long time since I had one of those from you, Mac,' observed a happy recipient of a leg-side full toss. 'It'll be a sight longer before you get another,' snapped Macaulay.

In his last season of bowling authority Macaulay found ideal conditions for his off-spin when Yorkshire played Northamptonshire at Kettering. The pitch was drying swiftly in sunshine after night rain and the Northamptonshire captain, V. W. C. Jupp, was delayed in arrival at the ground. He was informed that a deputy had won the toss and chosen first innings.

Northamptonshire were all out for 27 and the gleeful Macaulay took seven wickets for nine runs. Jupp was also an off-break bowler and Yorkshire lost their first two wickets for four runs, as promise of further sensational cricket. It came. The Kettering boundary is short and Herbert Sutcliffe hit 10 sixes in an innings of 112.

With more than ten years of county experience and two tours of Australia behind him Maurice Leyland came to the peak of his powers in 1934. It was not the year of his highest aggregate for Yorkshire because he was wanted five times by England, for whom he made 109 at Lord's, 153 at Old Trafford and 110 at the Oval, but his cricket had reached maturity without losing the eagerness of approach that made him a favourite of crowds everywhere.

No more contented cricketer than Leyland ever lived. He enjoyed home seasons, he enjoyed tours. 'They can pick me,' he said on hearing of some player's uncertain availability, 'I'll always go.'

Go he did; to Australia, South Africa, West Indies and on

coaching engagements to India. He was ready for cricket whenever the summers came round. He was a player with a strong sense of occasion, as adaptable to Test match as to Festival frolic.

He believed that the pleasures of cricket should involve spectators as well as players and that the game should not be deprived of humour even in its professional business. From the outfield he was prepared to share conversation with the crowd, which suited occupants of the Hill at Sydney. In a county match an opposing batsman was so comprehensively bowled that only one stump was left standing; as the batsman walked away Leyland strolled across from his nearby fielding position and respectfully laid the standing stump on the grass with the fallen.

At Bradford he had taken two wickets in successive balls and as the new batsman was on the way to the crease Leyland ostentatiously marked out a run-up at three times its normal length. His jokes were never unkind and always in context. He augmented the joy of cricket but never diminished its dignity.

He could please the spectators and at the same time fulfil his playing responsibilities because he was an exceptionally talented cricketer. He could afford to hit the ball hard because his batting methods were fundamentally sound. To the customary strength of the left-hander on the leg side he added a beautiful and uncommonly powerful off-drive.

Sound technique was the basis of his Test-match success. He simply reduced the proportion of speculative strokes and trusted to a well-organised defence until the bowling permitted scoring opportunities. Against Australia he made seven centuries and averaged over 50.

In all his cricket, for country, county or club, he made the game interesting through his happy approach. His temperament was equable, his resolution was manifest and his courage was never in question. Questioned on his reaction to fast, short-pitched bowling he gave the honest admission: 'Nobody likes it, but some show their dislike more than others.'

Leyland had all-round ability. He was left-handed as bowler and as batsman and would no doubt have developed in orthodox spin at slow-medium pace but for the presence of Rhodes and Kilner in the Yorkshire side.

His later bowling, occasional rather than regular, introduced the 'chinaman'—bowled with the leg-break action by a left-hander—which added to the gaiety of the game through bewilderment of batsmen or rapid scoring when sharpness of spin was not accompanied by accuracy of length.

Defeating the batsman or being hit for six, dismissed for 0 or completing his century, Maurice Leyland saw cricket as the only conceivable way of life for him.

18

Prosperity and pleasure

Bowes and Verity served as lynch-pins of Yorkshire authority to the interruption of cricket at the end of 1939. They were first and second in the county bowling averages for six successive seasons and the whole scheme of Yorkshire's attack was constructed round them.

Their presence was both a help and a handicap to the supporting bowlers of the time, who found that though they gained from association with success they were also limited in opportunity. Bowes was inevitably given the end most favourable to fast bowling, Verity the spin bowler's choice.

In these circumstances no other bowler came to greatness for Yorkshire during the period, but important secondary parts were taken by Frank Smailes, Cyril Turner and Ellis Robinson.

Smailes was brought into the side as a new-ball bowler, right-arm of fast-medium pace, and he proved that he could also reduce speed and find effectiveness with off-breaks. Taking over 100 wickets in four seasons and 96 in 1935 he met requirements admirably and in 1939 he achieved a performance denied to many of the very greatest bowlers. He took all 10 wickets in an innings.

He was also a hard-hitting left-handed batsman, inconsistent by the nature of his method but reaching his 1,000 runs in 1938 and scoring three centuries. In 1938 he was invited to Old Trafford for the final selection of the England team against Australia, but the side was never chosen because the match was washed away in four days of downpour. His consolation England cap came in 1946 when he played against India at Lord's.

Cyril Turner, like Smailes, was not a leading Yorkshire player but a significant and valued member of outstanding teams. Turner, too, was a right-arm bowler and left-hand batsman and his functions were rather less specific than those of Smailes. He served as middle-order batsman and change bowler of medium pace, with his invaluable service as a reliable man-of-all-work. If necessary he could swing the new ball; in emergency he could open the innings; he was always a willing 'nightwatchman'; he was skilful in defence and defiant in spirit when an innings was under threat of collapse.

Circumstances gave him more scope for batting than for bowling. He reached 1,000 runs once, in 1934, but he never took 100 wickets in a season. What he did do, which brought him deep appreciation from Yorkshire, was to make himself into one of the finest fieldsmen in the country.

He was competent in any position, but distinction came in the 'suicide squad' of those who came a yard or two nearer to the bat than was either customary or healthy and so created catches and the sense of enclosure that oppressed so many opposing batsmen.

E. P. Robinson, who was a south Yorkshireman and not related to Emmott, first played in 1934 and established his position in 1937 when he took 78 wickets. Long and strong fingers gave him exceptional powers of spin in slow-medium off-breaks, though his virtues were sometimes obscured in uncertainty of length and direction which added excitement to life in the leg-trap. In return, Ellis Robinson was prepared to take his turn dangerously near to the bat, where he held some remarkable diving catches.

After one of them, which left Robinson full length on the ground, breathless from the impact with earth, Mitchell moved over from a nearby station, looked down at Robinson and murmured in congratulation: 'Get up; you're making an exhibition of yourself.' Yorkshire were genuinely proud of each other, but effusive praise was not in their nature.

Robinson, who made a third member of the side to bowl right-handed and bat left-handed, usually played a brief innings through attempts to hit the ball out of sight, but Yorkshire were rarely dependent on the batting of Nos 10 and 11.

In the season after the retirement of Percy Holmes a 17-

year-old named L. Hutton was given his first game. In 1936 N. W. D. Yardley played in a few matches during his Cambridge University vacation. P. A. Gibb had been introduced a year earlier, with qualifications as both batsman and wicket-keeper. In a cricketing period of exceptionally well-prepared pitches Yorkshire were never at a loss for batting recruits.

Bowling and fielding were the decisive factors in championship success but trustworthy batting supplied the necessary scope in time and runs. Throughout the 1930s Yorkshire were a notably efficient batting side and the period was one of memorable batting.

The period was, indeed, one of cricket's most satisfying and prosperous periods. The professional player and the county cricket team held a high ranking in sport, attendances and memberships increased—for the more prominent counties at least—and pitches in first-class standard encouraged enterprising and skilful play. There was, undoubtedly, a wide margin between the strongest and weakest teams, but a county-cricket career was an ambition and a treasured possession.

Yorkshire were a side of strong loyalty to each other as individuals and to their traditions as a team. Inevitably men of such forthright character fell into occasional disagreement among themselves, but to a privileged observer the dressing-room harmony was remarkable; help for any player out of form or enduring a run of misfortune was always forthcoming and community response to any challenge from outside was immediate and unanimous.

Yorkshire gave batsmen as well as bowlers to England. Sutcliffe played in his last Test match in 1935, standing down at Headingley because of injury and failing to regain a place, though his omission from the M.C.C. tour of Australia in 1936-7 was viewed with scorn in Yorkshire and misgiving in wider fields. Even with increasing stiffness of movement Sutcliffe managed to find his way towards or beyond 2,000 runs until the time of retirement.

Barber and Mitchell both came to Test-match honours in 1935, Barber with selection at Headingley during a spell of particularly impressive form, Mitchell as a last-minute substitute in the same match.

Barber deserved his England cap but he was a county rather than an international cricketer by method and temperament. He was a handsome batsman, small in stature but upright in style with a liking for the off-drive. He was happier in the routine situation than in crisis and he preferred the trustworthy pitch to the turning ball, but in his unassertive way he fitted neatly into Yorkshire's pattern and could be relied on for his 1,000 runs a season. He was not often in debt when he began his innings, for he not only saved runs in the outfield but was rarely at fault in catching.

Arthur Mitchell was a more forthright cricketing character. As a batsman he was greatly skilled and entirely devoted to the immediate needs of his side. Circumstances ruled his approach: he could supply grim defence or concentrated hitting. When neither was particularly required he tended to follow business-like rather than relaxed batting, making life easier for others more than for himself.

The extreme contrasts of his range were startling. In his most famous defensive innings he drew the wrath of crowd and critics at Old Trafford by staying for six hours to score 123 and to disguise by his resolution and superb judgement the evil in a dry and sandy pitch that subsequently gave Macaulay a bowling triumph.

His own benefit match at Bradford illustrated his hitting powers, for when Yorkshire had been set 199 to score in an hour and threequarters for victory over Surrey, Mitchell joined Sutcliffe in a partnership raising 105 in 55 minutes. Bradford and Mitchell's hitting also provided a classic misunderstanding. A trophy known as the Lawrence Gold Cup sweetened by 100 guineas was awarded for some years in acknowledgement of the fastest individual 100 of the season. Yorkshiremen were also acquainted with a local beer marketed under the label of 'Gold Cup'.

Mitchell was hitting magnificently because Yorkshire needed quick runs. The day was warm. As Mitchell's personal score was mounting towards the century Leyland came down the pitch between overs to offer the gentle reminder, 'What about the Gold Cup?

'I could do with one,' replied Mitchell, pushing aside his cap to wipe sweat from his brow.

Mitchell's first Test against South Africa in 1935 exemplified his batting versatility.

He came dramatically into the match because Leyland reported unfit an hour or two before the start of play. Yorkshire were without an engagement and Mitchell was brought from his Baildon home to Headingley in a motor-car ride that gave him little time to consider the possibilities of the day.

By lunchtime he was batting, helping England to recover from a poor start as dampness dried from the pitch. Mitchell stayed for three hours to score 58. In their second innings (of a three-day match) England were required to score quickly to force an advantage and Mitchell was sent in first with Smith of Derbyshire. 128 runs were made in less than two hours before a wicket fell and Mitchell's contribution to the innings was an enterprising 72.

From that splendid beginning Mitchell's Test career should have been assured, but fortune ran against him. He had to drop out of the fourth Test because of injury and though he scored 40 in his one innings at the Oval opportunity never returned. In the following seasons of 1936 and 1937 India and New Zealand were the tourists and the Test selectors turned experimentally towards younger batsmen.

Mitchell undertook two overseas tours, one for England to India in 1933–4 under D. R. Jardine and one for Yorkshire to Jamaica in the early months of 1936.

The Yorkshire tour was at the request of the Jamaica Cricket Association, involving a programme of six matches. Yorkshire could not send their full championship side because Sellers had business commitments at home, Yardley could not miss a Cambridge University term and Barber was touring New Zealand with M.C.C.

Paul Gibb was appointed captain and George Hirst went as umpire and to share managerial duties with Herbert Sutcliffe. In meeting the full Jamaican side three times, in matches extending over five days, Yorkshire were responding to a formidable challenge, for Jamaica had not lost a home match in 10 years.

They lost to Yorkshire. In the first of the three major engagements Jamaica scored 280 and 257, Yorkshire 325 and 214 for five wickets. Mitchell's innings were 66 and 101 not out. In the second match Jamaica were made to follow on but Yorkshire could not dismiss them twice; in the third match the batting was overwhelming, Yorkshire's 556 for nine wickets finally conceding advantage to Jamaica's 592.

19

Special occasions

Yorkshire were so masterful in the championship of 1935 that their one defeat would have been a notable event of the season even without its dramatic circumstances. The match was played at Huddersfield immediately preceding the August Bank Holiday weekend. Essex were the visitors, the weather was fine and the metaphorical thunderbolt was entirely unexpected.

Mitchell and Smailes were out of the side because of injuries, but as Essex had already been overwhelmed at Colchester Yorkshire entered the match and took first innings without the slightest misgiving. They found a pitch of exceptional pace and bowlers to take advantage of the conditions. In an hour Yorkshire were all out for a total of 31. H. D. Read had taken six wickets for 11 runs, M. S. Nichols four for 17.

Read played only briefly in first-class cricket but his fast bowling was so impressive in 1935 that it brought him to the England team in the last Test match. Nichols was one of the most industrious and successful all-rounders in his time. Wednesday, July 31st, 1935, was his day of days. Having taken morning wickets he occupied afternoon and evening with an innings of 146 and returned to the ground on Thursday to take seven wickets in a second dismissal of Yorkshire for less than 100 during a morning.

Yorkshire recovered breath in the day and a half left spare and recovered balance at the weekend against Lancashire, who were put out for 53 at Bradford, mainly by Bowes, who returned six wickets for 16 runs. He took another six wickets in the follow-on, though at much greater trouble and cost, because Watson, batting adventurously at arm's length, so to speak, hit 25 boundaries in scoring 141.

That game was a Yorkshire satisfaction but not the most memorable victory of the season.

In early June Kent came to Bradford to play on a spin bowler's pitch. The first day brought two completed innings, of 182 by Kent and 131 by Yorkshire. On the second morning Woolley was sent in first to receive any benefit the rolling had given and in 65 minutes he conjured 73 runs from bowlers striving desperately to restrain him until the pitch turned awkward again.

The first Kent wicket was taken at 107, the last at 140. Yorkshire needed 192 to win. Their innings was virtually Sutcliffe against the spin of Freeman and the slow left-hander Lewis. All through the afternoon the match remained absorbingly balanced. Each little partnership gave Yorkshire a prospect of victory, each wicket taken raised the hopes of Kent. Yorkshire at 120 for six seemed in desperate straits, for though Sutcliffe was not out Sellers was notoriously uncertain against spin. Sellers hit a six and two fours to indicate his spirit. After tea Sutcliffe reached his 100 and play had to be suspended in the turmoil of acclamation.

At 185 for six Yorkshire were relaxing and at 185 Sutcliffe (not relaxing) was leg-before. Verity was bowled first ball. Sellers swept the final boundary. The batting of Sutcliffe and Woolley, the bowling of Verity and Macaulay and of Freeman and Lewis, splendid catches and inspired ground fielding and the prolonged tension of uncertainty, made cricket of the highest character.

In 1936 Derbyshire took the championship, leaving Yorkshire in third position and probably more disturbed by muscular strains that handicapped Bowes through much of the season than by loss of honours. In 1937 Yorkshire came to the top again, hotly pursued by Middlesex under R. W. V. Robins. The issue remained open to the last matches in the programme and public interest was augmented when in mid-August Robins sent Sellers a telegram to initiate a September challenge match to be played whatever the championship outcome.

Yorkshire had to struggle for their season's successes because their bowling power was seriously reduced through the absences of Bowes with knee injury. He was able to make few appearances before the end of June and in the early part of their programme Yorkshire found themselves spending long periods in the field.

In one week of May they scored 492 against Warwickshire and 465 against Sussex yet were behind on first innings and Leicestershire ran up a total of 458 at Hull after Yorkshire had declared at 523 for three. Bowes was back in the side for the match that had to be won to make sure of top place and he took six wickets for 36 runs in Hampshire's first innings at Bournemouth. That was enough; Yorkshire's batting established adequate advantage.

Twice in the championship programme the batting was overcome. Middlesex won by an innings at Lord's where the pace of Smith on the first day and the spin of Sims on the third showed Yorkshire in poor light. At Sheffield Verity experienced one of his few failures, missing the opportunity of conditions helpful enough to allow Lancashire's left-hander, Iddon, to take nine wickets for 42 runs in Yorkshire's second innings.

1937 brought fulfilment to all the bold prophecies advanced on behalf of Leonard Hutton. He had been introduced in 1934 and as an 18-year-old had been shrewdly protected against physical overstrain. In 1935 he remained an apprentice, playing 23 innings for 577 runs and a full season in 1936 clearly taxed his strength. He made 1,282 runs but his primary concern was the acquisition of batting experience and physical stamina.

1937 brought him to his 21st birthday, England status and the top of the Yorkshire averages with 62.76 for 2,448 runs.

His possession of the necessary health and strength for a cricketing career might have been questioned but his playing capacity was never in doubt. Sutcliffe wrote of him in 1935: 'He is the discovery of a generation—a certainty for a place as England's opening batsman.' George Hirst, speaking as Yorkshire's coach, said of the 16-year-old Hutton: 'There is nothing I can teach him.'

To any discerning eye Hutton did from the first display an astonishing mastery of technique. He had to wait for experience and strength, but he knew how to wait. He was neither impatient nor conceited.

Better health, following a tonsils operation, and the 'feel' of first-class cricket permitted him to show his talent in full flower. Before the end of June in 1937 he had collected six centuries, including 102 in a Test Trial and 136, 271 not out and 153 in successive innings for Yorkshire. Sutcliffe found only one cause for disappointment in him. At Hull against Leicestershire they had put on 315 together for the first wicket in four hours and 40 minutes when Hutton allowed himself to be bowled. Sutcliffe was thinking of a partnership of 556, at least.

Hutton's 10th century of the 1937 season was made in the Challenge Match which was played at the Oval and scheduled for four days though it was completed in three, September 11, 13, 14. The Robins telegram brought immediate response from the Yorkshire team whose suggestion was a stake of £10 a man and public opinion was overwhelmingly in favour of the game.

The proposed sidestake received less approval, particularly from those who recalled cricket's early history, and the Yorkshire authority sanctioned the fixture on condition that the gate receipts were for charity and that the game should not be regarded as a precedent for regular challenges. The danger in redevelopment of money matches, with potential abuse, was too obvious to need much emphasis.

Poor weather could not prevent attendances producing a profit of £700 for charitable distribution but circumstances gave most of the cricketing advantages to one side. Yorkshire won the toss and batted on an easy-paced pitch for a first innings total of 401. They batted discreetly and were not dismissed until after lunch on the second day, Hutton and Mitchell laying the foundation for a big score with their second-wicket partnership of 172.

Middlesex met the new-ball bowling of Bowes and Smailes under gloomy skies and in heavy atmosphere and were predictably routed. They had lost six wickets for 63 when the evening thunderstorm broke to wash away the day's play.

Further cricket was not possible until after lunch on the third day and Yorkshire briefly showed unexpected and unintentional mercy. They dropped so many catches that Middlesex were allowed to reach a total of 185.

In the follow-on, with the turf drying rapidly, sterner control was applied and Middlesex could stretch no further than 101, Verity taking eight wickets for 43 runs.

20

Credit and pride—and curtain

Yorkshire were champions of 1938 and 1939 well before the seasons ended. Middlesex were runners-up, as in 1937, but both the figures and general opinion gave Yorkshire a clear superiority and the manner of their cricket reflected credit on the players as it raised pride in the supporters.

The county strength was illustrated outside the championship as well as in it. Bradman's Australians were brought close to defeat before rain ended the match at Sheffield and in the fifth Test no fewer than five Yorkshire players were called to England service.

Success was not unbroken. The years brought six defeats, two in 1938 and four in 1939, but against these could be set 40 outright victories in 60 engagements and the maintenance of a reputation for confident and skilful cricket in the highest range. Reputation was, indeed, a fourth weapon added to the armoury of batting, bowling and fielding, for few counties approached their games against Yorkshire with optimism.

Yorkshire were a tremendous force in the cricket of the time. Membership rose to record levels and had to be limited by rule. Nearly 208,000 spectators paid turnstile admission money in 1938 and the Australian match of that year drew 35,000 spectators to the first day's play at Bramall Lane. In their away fixtures Yorkshire usually attracted the biggest attendance of the year to grounds they visited and through the summer the team received many more social invitations than there were days in which to fulfil them. Theatres, evening sports gatherings, golf courses, private hospitalities were all available to the team wherever they were playing. They fulfilled dinner-jacket obligations and they enlivened evenings in the four-ale bar.

Their cricket was a paramount concern. They accepted disciplines that applied equally to senior and junior members of the side. They shared team successes without trace of personal jealousies and on the field they gave all possible practical help to each other and to any newcomer in the team. Being Yorkshiremen, they disguised their compliments in mock-complaint and were firm in preservation of individual characters. Yorkshire's cricketers trusted each other and their cricket gained enormously from the mutual respect for differing, yet complementary abilities.

At one time or another in 1938 the list of first-team players had to be extended beyond the normal. Bowes and Smailes had to nurse strains, Mitchell missed some of the early matches and Turner played only 24 championship innings because no sooner had he recovered from an injury suffered in the leg-trap than he was taken to hospital with a broken nose from a batting accident.

The visit to Lord's for the July match with Middlesex cost Hutton a broken finger. Leyland a broken thumb and Gibb a split head, the pitch on the first day showing itself lively beyond all calculation. Yorkshire were defeated. A week later they were defeated again, by Surrey at the Oval where Hutton, Leyland and Gibb were absent because of the injuries and Verity, Bowes and Yardley had been called to the fourth Test.

These defeats were no more than a pause in Yorkshire's advance to the championship. Before Lord's they had already won eleven matches, six in successive engagements, and after the Oval they won six games out of the next seven to make sure of the honours of the season. They finished their programme with two more victories in case anyone should question their authority.

Their highest single achievement of the year was, however, outside the championship. They played the Australians at Sheffield during a period of broken weather, giving pitch conditions more to the liking of Yorkshire than of the Australians.

Yorkshire made immediate challenge by sending in the Australians, but the direct outcome was not particularly encouraging to the county supporters. Bradman applied himself to unfamiliar and unwelcome conditions and scored 59. Hassett

Bill Bowes bowling in 1934

Hedley Verity is recognised as one of the greatest ever bowlers, even although his career lasted only 10 years

The Yorkshire team of 1937. Left to right—Verity, Bowes, Yardley, Sellers, Sutcliffe, Smailes, Barber, Wood, Leyland, Turner and Hutton

Freddie Trueman, Yorkshire's controversial fast bowler who retired in 1968, holding the record of 307 Test match wickets

Norman Yardley, a past captain of Yorkshire and England

The 1951 Yorkshire team. Left to right, they are Hutton, Trueman, Leadbeater, Wilson, Brennan, Yardley, Appleyard, Watson, Wardle, Lester, Halliday

played an innings of notable skill and enterprise to hit three sixes and twelve fours in scoring 94.

The Australians made 222 in their first innings, Yorkshire 205. In the second Australian innings, played in the afternoon and evening of a cloudy Monday, on a pitch still damp, bowling raised itself to meet Yorkshire's highest hopes. Bowes was so masterful that 18 overs cost him no more than 28 runs, mostly edged. The dominant skill of the day was his but the luck was against him; he had Badcock and Bradman missed in the slips and he took only two wickets.

Bradman was in such difficulties against late swing that at one point in his innings he offered his bat resignedly to the nearby Yorkshire captain, saying, 'How *do* you play this stuff?'

Bowes bowled for the profit of others. In an atmosphere of almost terrifying excitement the last six Australian wickets went down for 32 runs and Yorkshire were left to make 150 to win.

The third morning brought more dark, damp weather and the early fall of Wood and Verity who had opened the innings overnight when time would have permitted an over or two, but rain did not. Sutcliffe and Hutton stayed together for an hour, offering no speculative stroke, prising their runs from reluctant Australians. From a slight misjudgement of the turning ball Hutton was caught at short leg. Sutcliffe and Barber were not out at lunch, Yorkshire 83 for three wickets.

There the cricket ended, but not the excitement, nor the splendour of the match. Spectators huddled into shelter during a lunchtime downpour and waited hopefully through an afternoon of further shower and fine interval. Eventual inspection of the saturated turf by Sellers and Bradman re-kindled vision of a Yorkshire victory. Sellers answered all speculation, spared Bradman any tactical problem with one decisive gesture to denote 'Match Abandoned'. He could never have made a more heartbreaking decision with greater firmness.

The Australians saw no more of Yorkshire as a team in 1938 but under a different cap they had some reason to feel that England was but Yorkshire writ large. Hutton was a batsman and Verity a bowler to be named without selectorial discussion and for the fifth Test, which had to be won if England were to share the rubber, Hutton, Verity, Bowes and Leyland were all in the first choice of team. On the eve of the match England found themselves without a wicketkeeper, Ames having injured a finger, and an emergency call was put out for Arthur Wood.

He came—to occupy himself as a privileged spectator until the third day. Hutton scored 364, Leyland scored 187 (run out) and Wood was required to enter into his first activity for England as a No. 8 batsman, going to the crease when the total was 770 for six.

He scored 53, shared a century partnership in 90 minutes and was caught and bowled from a full toss. Back in the dressing-room, in solemn-faced condemnation for his own mis-hit, he observed: 'Just the sort of thing I would do—in a crisis.'

Arthur Wood was close to his 40th birthday when he gained his first England cap, but he held his England place through the Test series of 1939 and was showing no marked loss of form when cricket was interrupted. He was not expected to play again after the six-season interval, but he returned happily to the Yorkshire side when a substitute was required for several matches in 1946.

Arthur Wood was proudly and devotedly a professional cricketer. He enjoyed playing and he enjoyed the summer life. Team-companions appreciated him as a competent technician who filled a difficult part in a bowling scheme that relied so much on catches from the edge of the bat and they also gave him licence to wear cap and bells in the light relief desirable to balance the intense concentration applied to business on the field.

Wood's wicketkeeping was soundly based, but he gave it a flourish that pleased the spectators without reducing efficiency. If a leg-side catch could be completed with a spectacular roll no harm was done, except to Wood's own laundry bills, and the day's play was made a little brighter.

His batting was undertaken with the same regard for public satisfaction. He was an exhibitionist by design more than by nature and indulgence in the improbable stroke tended to disguise a batting ability above the average. He could and did make his 1,000 runs in a season, but he was always a willing sacrifice to team needs before individual desires.

Although the inevitable periods of poor form distressed him more than he would confess he never showed resentment towards the fortune or success of others and he was as ready in expression of genuine praise as he was quick in appropriate comment.

H. B. Cameron, the South African, hit Verity for 30 runs in one over at Sheffield and Wood proffered consolation:

'You've got him in two minds now, Hedley.'

'What do you mean?'

'He doesn't know whether to hit you for four or for six.'

During an innings of 188 at Bradford, Woolley hit seven sixes, subjecting the football stand to heavy barrage.

'Sounds as though a Boy Scout band is going by,' observed Wood. 'Rat-a-tat-tat, Rat-a-tat-tat.'

Wood's last full season, 1939, was not one of his best with the bat but his wicketkeeping form kept him in the England side throughout the series against West Indies and in the county championship he caught 38 and stumped 27.

Yorkshire were beaten four times during the season but they won 20 matches and were champions before the programme came to its clouded end. Some of their performances were no less than magnificent and the side suggested increasing rather than diminishing power as the younger players developed and the older retained enviable ability.

Hutton was the leading batsman, with an average of 60 and an aggregate of 2,167 in championship engagements, but Sutcliffe, aged 44, averaged 50 and was in such wonderful form before injuries beset him that he had reached 1,000 runs by mid-June and had played four sucessive innings of 163, 116, 234 not out, and 175.

The 116 was made at Sheffield in an opening partnership of 315 that led to a total of 493 for one wicket, declared against Hampshire. The 234 was a share of 500 for seven, declared, against Leicestershire at Hull. The 175 was contribution to Yorkshire's 430 for five, declared, against Middlesex at Lord's.

Yorkshire won seven of their first eight championship fixtures and in this period completed only four of their innings. They declared six times, won five matches by an innings and beat Essex at Ilford with a fourth innings of 237 for three wickets. Interruption to success came at Bradford, where they were generous in offer to Gloucestershire.

The first day was lost to rain and after batting of persistent enterprise by both sides Yorkshire declared on the third afternoon leaving 100 minutes for play and 189 runs as a Gloucestershire target. Barnett set his sights accurately, hitting four sixes and eight fours as he scored 90 in an hour, and Gloucestershire won by six wickets with five minutes to spare.

Even more exciting—and satisfying because no declaration was involved—was the match at Stourbridge. Sunshine after rain on a pitch of natural response to the weather gave bowlers a birthday. Worcestershire were all out for 102 before the first lunchtime; Yorkshire had been dismissed for 91 by tea. In their second innings Worcestershire recovered from 41 for seven to 118 all out and at the second-day lunch Yorkshire, needing 130, were 77 for seven.

Leyland was their prop and stay and even with the last man as his partner could envisage victory. At 113 he hit a fierce, skimming drive towards long-off where the fieldsman had time to sink to his knees for better sighting of the catch, if not for prayer. Worcestershire had won.

Yorkshire's bowlers of the year were Verity, Bowes and the rapidly improving Robinson, whose sharp off-breaks still occasioned some trepidation in the leg-trap though his accuracy of length and direction had become more trustworthy. The bowling feat of the year, however, was achieved by Smailes who carried heavy responsibility in the Derbyshire match at Sheffield because Bowes and Verity were playing for England.

Yorkshire batted first and were all out for 83, which no doubt caused some embarrassment to Hutton, Wood, Verity and Bowes in the England dressing-room at Lord's. Retort was available to them within the hour. Derbyshire were all out for 20. Smailes had taken four wickets for 11 runs, Smurthwaite, a right-hander of medium pace, five wickets for seven runs.

Breathing thanks and relief, Yorkshire's batsmen, led by

Barber with 100, made 310 and then delivered Derbyshire over to Smailes. In 18 overs he took all 10 wickets, for 47 runs.

By the time of the final southern tour, comprising engagements at Dover, Bournemouth and Brighton, the country was in turmoil of preparations for war. Remarkable cricket was played and scarcely roused remark because even for spectators it was only at the back of the mind and communications spreading sports news were in confusion. Telephoned reports were often hours delayed; telegraphed reports were handed to Post Office messengers to find delivery without mishap or to disappear completely in the process of transmission.

After the first day's play at Dover, in which Yorkshire had scored 338, with a Hutton century, the four cricket writers representing Yorkshire newspapers were in their hotel lounge at about 10 p.m. A telephone call was received from the *Sheffield Daily Telegraph* to the effect that no account of Yorkshire's cricket had arrived, though it had, as usual, been sent by Press Telegram from the ground at close of play.

A large space in the sports page was waiting and could the correspondent please dictate some material to fill it. The correspondent was willing, but in difficulty; he had left his brief-case containing notes and scorecard at the ground.

Co-operation saved the situation. The *Telegraph* correspondent stayed on the telephone (fearful lest a call broken should never be re-connected) dictating an account of the cricket fed to him sentence by sentence as colleagues improvised, one memory refreshed by another. The column was filled.

After the feverishness of Dover, where motor-cycle dispatch riders made a procession to the ground, Bournemouth carried a holiday-resort calm, though it was a calm of unreality and the military world impinged with papers for the call-up of Herbert Sutcliffe, who was on the Reserve of Officers. Yorkshire won at Bournemouth by an innings as they had won at Dover, and were sure of another championship.

They travelled on to Brighton, cricket continuing because no authority had stopped it. The match was well attended, partly no doubt because it was for the benefit of James Parks, partly because prearranged routines remained in existence.

Batsmen went to the crease, bowlers bowled, spectators assembled and applauded and nobody felt that cricket mattered in the least.

Play was not casual, watching was not indifferent, but behind the bowling and batting lay concern for plans and prospects in another way of life. Cox lit the cricketing twilight with an innings of 198 in which he hit one six and 38 fours and the Sussex 387 was topped by Yorkshire's 392, Hutton and Yardley making centuries. Fine weather broke on the second evening and Sussex played their second innings on a softened pitch. It was completed in less than 12 overs for a total of 33 and Verity's last bowling analysis in first-class cricket was o 6 m 1 r 9 w 7.

21

The men of management

Through the two world wars the Yorkshire County Cricket Club remained in being, without attempting any of its normal functions. No county matches were arranged, no officials were elected or re-elected, but an administration was maintained to deal with such business as arose, including receipt of some subscriptions in the nominal form of donations.

In the period of the 1914-18 war Lord Hawke was President and F. C. Toone was Secretary. As both were above the age acceptable for active military service their contribution to the fighting forces was made in the form of welfare organisation. The County Cricket Club offices in Leeds became headquarters for the West Riding Volunteers, with Lord Hawke as adjutant and Toone his secretarial assistant. Toone also served through some of the war years in the Special Constabulary, resigning, of necessity, when he received official military status in the Volunteers.

Frederick Toone was the third secretary of the Yorkshire club, though the first, George Padley, held office for only one year. The second secretary was J. B. Wostinholm, whose activities over 38 years were more of a labour of love than a professional undertaking. When he began, in 1864, his remuneration was 10 per cent of the subscription income; in 1870 he was advanced to a salary, or fee, of £10 per annum and by 1882 he was being paid 25 guineas a year.

When Wostinholm announced retirement in 1903 the post was advertised, at £350 p.a., and F. C. Toone, for five years secretary of Leicestershire, was appointed. Toone had impressed Lord Hawke, by this time both President and captain of Yorkshire, and in Toone's period of office, which ended with his death in 1930, President and Secretary lived in close harmony, with no question raised of the dominant influence.

Toone was a skilful organiser and a persuasive advocate for the club, building a membership that was beyond 6,000 by 1930. His competence, seniority among county secretaries and the influence of Lord Hawke in M.C.C. brought him appointment as manager of three successive tours to Australia and his contributions to these undertakings were noted with a knighthood. He became Sir Frederick Toone after the 1928-9 tour in which Chapman's team won the Ashes.

On Toone's appointment in 1903 Yorkshire moved administrative headquarters from Sheffield to Leeds. Sheffield's numerical dominance of the county committee had already been reduced and the geographical advantages of Leeds were so obvious that the change could be made without any derogatory reflection on the Sheffield members and officials.

The move to Leeds did not change Yorkshire's policy of match presentation. The club remained a county club without a ground of its own. Matches were spread to meet, as far as possible, the convenience of members and the needs of day-to-day supporters. Instead of committing themselves to the costs of ownership and development of one ground Yorkshire contributed towards the upkeep of several, believing that in this they could best encourage cricket throughout the county and also justify membership of a county organisation over the wide area.

After Sir Frederick Toone died in office Yorkshire appointed his young assistant, John H. Nash, to the secretaryship. The decision was not a formality. Nash was little known in cricket and there were many applications for the post. Lord Hawke expressed his view that an older man would be required to exercise the necessary authority in the county's internal organisation and in the wider councils of cricket. Subsequently convinced of his mistaken impression Lord Hawke characteristically told the new secretary of original misgivings, acknowledged conversion and gave wholehearted approval and trust.

Toone had to work with only one President, Lord Hawke, over a period of 27 years. Nash served three Presidents within a generation.

Lord Hawke died, aged 78, in the autumn of 1938 and was

succeeded by Sir Stanley Jackson. Lord Hawke had made Yorkshire cricket in particular and cricket in general the preoccupation of a lifetime and could justly be rated the greatest single influence Yorkshire cricket ever knew. He could be dogmatic and obstructive but his affections were genuine and his principles were never disguised in pragmatism. He lived long enough to believe that all change was not necessarily for the better, but he was himself an innovator and a visionary in the limited sphere of his activities.

As a captain he knew his players, the needs of his players and what, in his view, would be of benefit to his players and he was steadfast in the pursuit of his objectives. Time and time again he insisted that the paid player would respond to professional respect with professional integrity. His lasting service to cricket was not the development of wage-scales, winter pay and benefit funds, but the creation of professional pride.

As a President he was a forthright leader. He never sought to avoid the debatable decision and his speeches at Yorkshire's annual meetings were anticipated with lively interest by members attending and by the wider public reached through newspaper reports. The drama usually developed from personal asides to the prepared pronouncements.

Noting the extension of Test matches in England to four days of play he added, 'There is danger of turning Test matches into a fetish.' He condemned the 'freak declarations' of 1932 not on grounds of their ingenuity but because unintended interpretation of the rules by arrangement was, he felt, contrary to the spirit of the game. His reluctance to approve the challenge match of 1937 between Middlesex and Yorkshire was based on the fear of a revival of matches for money stakes, which had once led cricket into disrepute and disharmony.

In 1925 a casual phrase became a label attached for ever to Lord Hawke's name and reputation. England were losing a Test rubber in Australia and newspaper comment under the name of Cecil Parkin, the Lancashire bowler who was not on the tour, suggested that England would fare better with a professional player as captain. 'Pray God no professional shall ever captain England!' exclaimed Lord Hawke.

He elaborated by saying that cricket would be the poorer were amateur cricketers no longer available to captain, but inevitably the startling phrase made the headlines and its qualification was obscured.

Sir Stanley Jackson, diplomat by training, was never likely to become embroiled in controversy and as Yorkshire's President he had little opportunity. Through six of his eight years in office county cricket was in suspension.

The club remained in being, with an improvised secretariat when J. H. Nash was on active service overseas, and Sir Stanley Jackson made it his business to keep in contact with the office and the scattered players. He was able to welcome the reassembly of 1946 and share the satisfaction of another championship won, but early in 1947 he was involved in a road accident and consequent shock led to his death before the cricket season began.

T. L. Taylor was appointed President for the remainder of the year and re-elected by members from 1948 to 1960, the year of his death. T. L. Taylor had his home and business interests in Leeds and was able to make the county cricket club his close personal concern. He was shrewd in management and respected by the players for both his knowledge of the game and for his frequent appearances at matches and practices.

In his period Yorkshire negotiated a long lease for use of the Headingley ground to serve as county headquarters, but Sir William A. Worsley had become President before the building of new dressing-rooms, secretarial offices and an indoor practice shed had been completed.

In the summer of 1943 Captain Hedley Verity of the Green Howards died of wounds in the military hospital at Caserta, near Naples. He was 38 years old.

Verity's first-class cricket career was confined to the seasons between 1930 and 1939 and in that period he established himself among the greatest players in the whole history of the game. In aggregate his achievements could not compare with those of longer career, but his performances gave measure of his quality.

He took 1,956 wickets, 144 of them in Test matches; against the 1934 Australians at Lord's he took 15 wickets in the match,

14 in one day. In every full season for Yorkshire he never failed to reach 100 wickets and twice he took all 10 in an innings. He became an England bowler in his first full year of first-class cricket and he was an unquestioned choice for the tour of Australia a year later.

Verity's death cost Yorkshire and England more than the loss of an outstanding player. It took from cricket a textbook of the professional code of conduct and performance. Verity counted cricket both a privilege and an obligation and bowling a proper subject for serious study. With the natural gifts of athleticism he would have found easy success by merely 'doing what comes naturally'. The height from which he delivered the ball would have given him 'lift' from the pitch without great effort on his part and as a left-hander he would have needed no more than gentle finger spin to make him menacing when the ball turned.

These facilities were no more than a basis of bowling for Verity. He used them as grammar for composition. He always wanted more than conquest without effort. His happiest bowling was against the most powerful challenge batsmen or circumstances could offer. To keep Bradman in anxiety for an hour meant more to him than a dramatic analysis conceded by ineffectual opponents.

At times he seemed more concerned with the study for its own sake than with the product of study and suggested that unless success came as a planned development it would represent a success diminished in value. He was prepared to bowl six overs to force a return catch rather than scatter speculative bait through two overs for a possible mis-hit to cover.

When conditions were entirely to the disadvantage of batsmen Verity took his triumphs almost perfunctorily, with the self-assurance that assumed success a formality. He dominated and dispatched. Rare indeed the occasion when he spurned a bowling favour or neglected an opportunity, but he was fascinated and inspired by any challenge to his skill and his wits. Where the pitch offered only a small area of untrustworthiness to be exploited, where subtlety of field-setting and prolonged accuracy of length and direction had to be preserved, where batsmen and bowler were competing at a high level of cricketing ingenuity, there Verity found the highest satisfaction in the art that was his business.

His absorption with the task in hand, his power of intense concentration, gave him an air of detachment from triumph and discomfiture alike. He played in the context of the match, but he bowled in a remote world of his own thinking and endeavour. He gave little evidence of being either elated or downcast. He affected no mannerism, created no public 'character' for conscious display.

Had he survived to return to cricket he would have been immensely influential in a generation needing guidance by example. He would have presented patience, thoughtfulness and dedication as elements of bowling and he would have recommended cricket as an honourable occupation, to be undertaken with a resolve to seek its highest rewards through unflagging application. Hedley Verity never played cricket carelessly or inconsequentially; to him any match or part of a match was important to somebody.

22

Yielding place to new

In 1946, when the county championship was resumed, Yorkshire thankfully and nostalgically recalled old forces to serve as new. They played again under A. B. Sellers and reassembled Maurice Leyland, Bill Bowes, Wilfred Barber, Cyril Turner, Leonard Hutton, Frank Smailes, Norman Yardley, Paul Gibb and Ellis Robinson.

Verity was dead, Sutcliffe had put bat and pads away, Mitchell had become county coach, Wood in his 48th year could scarcely consider resumption of daily wicketkeeping.

War service and war years had stolen more than time from the cricketers. Bowes had spent three years in Italian and German prison camps and came back to cricket under clear medical warning that the fast bowling demands of younger days should never again be imposed on his physical captaincy. Head injuries in a transport accident contributed to a general deterioration in the health of Cyril Turner and his adoption of spectacles for cricket. Hutton had undergone several operations on a fractured left arm, which was left permanently shortened.

The old Yorkshire took one curtain call. They won the championship of 1946. They won it essentially as trustees of tradition and reputation because most of the regular players were within a season or two of final departure and only Hutton, Yardley, Gibb and Robinson had careers of any consequence ahead of them.

P. A. Gibb had been playing occasionally for Yorkshire since 1935, but no established place was open to him when Wood was wicketkeeper and the Yorkshire batting was already the envy of most counties. Gibb had developed his cricket in the distinguished company of Sir Julien Cahn's XI and had then gone up to Cambridge University where he was contemporary with Yardley. He played for Yorkshire when required, providing immediate evidence of his batting ability with an innings of 157 not out in his first championship match, and he also appeared in representative cricket for Scotland.

During the war Gibb served as a Royal Air Force pilot and afterwards personal circumstances and a passionate desire to concentrate his interests in cricket led him to turn professional. He played for Yorkshire in 1946 and toured Australia with M.C.C. in 1946–7 as an amateur and then joined Essex, who were seeking a wicketkeeper and batsman, as a professional.

Norman Yardley followed a conventional path to the highest honours of cricket. Outstanding as a schoolboy player, he fulfilled expectations at Cambridge where he was captain in 1938 and he played in his first Test match on tour in South Africa with Hammond's team in 1938-9. In 1939 he had a full season with Yorkshire, finding his best form in the later months when he made centuries against Warwickshire and Sussex.

Commissioned in the Green Howards, Yardley saw service in India, Iran and Egypt before taking part in the Sicily invasion that cost Verity his life. Yardley himself was wounded when the British forces reached the Italian mainland and spent nine months of 1944 in hospital, but a shattered ankle was repaired to permit a return to cricket and the development of a careeer that led to captaincy of England in 14 Tests and captaincy of Yorkshire for eight seasons.

Leonard Hutton never left England during the war but he suffered a serious injury, involving permanent disablement, in the Army Physical Training Corps. A complicated fracture of the left forearm demanded a series of operations and a shortening of the arm and Hutton has confessed that there were dark days in hospital when he could see no cricketing future for himself.

He was able to test the weakened arm in some improvised matches in 1945 and in 1946 batting was his business again.

He was an opening batsman for Yorkshire and for England in the three-match Test rubber against India. In an exceptionally wet summer he scored 1,552 runs and the limitations imposed by his weaker arm were scarcely to be noted except by himself and by the indication that he was no longer prepared to attempt the hook strokes against fast bowling.

Yorkshire in 1946 were not a side with glowing prospects. Early reconstruction was an obvious necessity and by the end of the season Leyland, Barber and Turner had given notice of retirement. Gibb accommodated a desire to stay in cricket to a change in personal circumstances by becoming a professional for Essex after he had toured Australia with Hammond's team. Fiddling, who had been a reserve wicketkeeper since 1938, took an engagement with Northamptonshire.

Further revision was enforced by illness. In 1946 the left-arm bowling vacancy had been filled by Arthur Booth, who, succeeding Verity, followed a player younger than himself. Booth first played for Yorkshire in 1931 but the dominance of Verity gave him little scope for regular appearances and he confined the bulk of his career to league engagements.

He was 43 years old when Yorkshire asked him for a full season's bowling and his response was to lead the county and the national averages with 111 wickets taken at a cost of 11.61 runs each. He was awarded his Yorkshire cap and with his economical method and wide experience of professional bowling could have expected three or four seasons in first-class cricket, but scarcely had the 1947 programme begun than he was overcome by rheumatic ailment that compelled an end to his county career.

Bowes played through 1947, taking a belated benefit that exceeded £8,000 as measure of thanks for services rendered, but he had made his retirement known before the last matches and after the season Sellers quietly passed on the captaincy to Yardley, though he agreed to act as deputy when Yardley was required by England in 1948.

Bowes could and did leave to the new generation of cricketers a legacy of bowling example but he could not offer them an illustration of himself in his most effective manner.

The young bowlers of the late 1940s and early 1950s were in the schoolroom when Bowes was devastating the weaker batsmen and harrying the strongest with lively pace and magnetic swing. They could marvel at figures in the record books but they could not derive inspiration from blazing fires because in 1946 and 1947 the flames were necessarily damped.

Bowes did show, as Verity would have shown, the fundamental features of great bowling to the cricketers willing to learn. He emphasised the skills of control, the need for concentrated effort over long periods, the attitude towards bowling as a purposeful occupation, infinite in variety to meet differing situations.

Sellers met unfamiliar problems in his last experience of captaincy. In 1932 he had taken over a side of established character, of high technical accomplishment and with a common interest clearly defined. He integrated himself and he contributed to the common welfare, but in a sense Yorkshire capained Sellers as much as Sellers captained Yorkshire. He led them as they desired to be led, with an outcome eminently satisfactory to both captain and captained.

As new players joined the side, one by one, they absorbed the prevailing atmosphere, acquired the existing outlook. After the war, when new players had to be introduced in haste and in numbers, the team's character was necessarily more complicated and less clearly defined. Lines of communication between seniors and juniors were uncertain. Recognised practices to some were unfamiliar requirements to others. Young postwar cricketers adventuring into first-class fields had to learn not only county cricket but also cricketing elements not instilled elsewhere.

Sellers was therefore surprised and dismayed to find himself teaching rudiments of catching and throwing and backing-up as well as the finer points of field-setting. He had to explain principles of running between wickets that came as novelty as distinct from ingrained habit. Yorkshire under reconstruction had to find cricketers capable of becoming first-class cricketers at a standard beyond their experience if not beyond their conception.

The experimental years brought inevitable disappointments by measure of both individual reactions and team achievements. 1947 saw a fall to eighth place in the final championship table and only once in 12 years could Yorkshire finish first and then, in 1949, the honour had to be shared.

In the period of rather desperate search, when as many as 26 different players were called on in one season and 'caps' were rather generously bestowed, Hutton carried an enormous weight of batting responsibility. His superb technique invited individous comparisons and Yorkshire took pride in his ability and performances, but noting his averages in 60s and 70s followers had cause to wonder why nobody else came within 20 runs of his figures.

In 1947 and 1949, particularly, were batting summers that gave Hutton 4,708 runs for Yorkshire alone. No other batsman reached 3,000 in the two seasons combined.

Political and economic factors of the time made team construction on a solid basis more difficult. Compulsory military service was still in force, delaying enrolment of players or interrupting the necessary apprenticeship in first-class sport and the urgent demands of industry reduced the comparative financial attraction of county cricket. Yorkshire were never short of recruits, but in Yorkshire, as elsewhere, there was disinclination to undertake the discipline that turns talent into consistent effectiveness.

Yorkshire finished fourth in the championship of 1948 but found basis for deep satisfaction only in the supremacy of Hutton. Three other batsmen, Watson, Halliday and Lester, scored over 1,000 runs but there was a disturbing lack of consistency and general assurance and too many of the Yorkshire innings were a speculation.

Bowling and fielding fell far below expectations and requirements. Smailes, in his last season, was an off-spinner rather than a new-ball force, and Coxon, admirable in his persistence, was without the pace to become a commanding fast bowler and without the control of action to develop reserves of authority for the days when conditions gave a batting advantage.

When Arthur Booth was compelled to give up first-class cricket J. H. Wardle became Yorkshire's choice as slow left-arm bowler. He came with the advantages of youth—he was

23 when he first played for the county—remarkable stamina and an unquestionable ability to spin the ball. Bowling nearly twice as many overs as any other bowler in 1948 he took 148 wickets and established himself firmly in the side, causing reservations only in occasional failure to make the most of opportunities and in lapses from the accuracy traditionally associated with bowlers of his type.

Yardley was saddled with a difficult period of captaincy. His own conceptions of cricket were based on the pre-war principle of individual responsibility towards a community cause. Personal achievement represented success or failure essentially in its contribution to team needs. Discipline came from within because the necessity for it was appreciated and respected.

Yardley was a shrewd tactician and a remarkably accurate judge of the likely behaviour in a pitch. As captain of Yorkshire and England he rarely misread a situation or pursued a plan without logic, but too often he was frustrated in his intent because of inadequate response. He could put on the appropriate bowler but could not prevent an untimely technical lapse in bowling. He could assess a batting situation but could not eliminate a careless stroke. He could set a field meticulously but could not insure against misfielding.

Yardley's aim in cricket was for purposeful play in a pleasant atmosphere with an outcome leaving no cause for recriminations. To him winning was important but not all-important, striving took precedence over achievement and discipline was the acceptance of obligations.

His own cricket was played on precisely those terms. In batting he gave a polish to natural talent through application of experience and thoughtfulness. In bowling he directed a much more limited ability with equal concentration to the immediate business on hand. He was a reliable fieldsman because to be otherwise would have been, in his view, a breach of trust. He was surprised rather than dismayed to discover that his cricketing philosophy was not universally held.

23

Doorway to disillusion

By 1950 Yorkshire's cricket had begun to see its way into the next decade. An accepted XI had not been constructed but eight players took part in more than 20 of the championship fixtures and Hutton and Yardley would have added to the number but for Test match calls and injuries.

An impressive opening partner for Hutton had been found in F. A. Lowson who made his second season memorable by scoring 2,000 runs. H. Halliday and J. V. Wilson rested comfortably among the batsmen with averages exceeding 40 and though the figures of E. Lester compared unfavourably with the previous season his value was measured, certainly by his captain, essentially in terms of capacity to change the course of a match.

Lowson had all the attributes of a Test-match cricketer, except perhaps the driving force of ambition, and he did play for England on the qualification of a sound method and a capacity to cope with most types of bowling. Halliday, Wilson and Lester had limitations as obvious as their merits.

Halliday's basis for batting was sound enough but his approach was inclined to be negative. He played a notably fine forcing shot past point from the back foot but when bowlers sought to contain him he accepted their dictation too readily and reduced himself to patient defence.

Wilson and Lester, in contrast, were happiest and most successful when they were attacking the bowling. Wilson, a left-hander, hit the ball with tremendous power, but he needed good form and good fortune because spin and swing exposed defensive weakness. Lester came to the county with a record of brilliant batting in club cricket at Scarborough and after scoring 657 runs in seven matches in 1947 he was induced to turn full-time professional.

Lester's batting was the product of trustworthy pitches at Scarborough and influenced by his club's tradition of enterprise. He was 25 years old when he found that some of the county bowling could be overcome with equal facility and his batting method had been formed.

Yorkshire welcomed him for the batsman he was, deprecating rather than encouraging any attempt to re-model his style. Against spin bowling of quality he remained manifestly vulnerable and his defensive limitations made his innings unpredictable but, in the words of Yardley, he was 'worth his weight in gold because he could change the course of a game in an hour'.

When he was in form and enjoying the fortune proverbially favouring the brave his batting was a delight to watch and a despair to oppose. He gave the impression of being able to drive anything between the long hop and the full toss. In the graph of his inconsistency were peaks of 24 Yorkshire centuries and he scored 10,616 runs for the county.

Both Lester and Wilson were assets in the field, Lester mainly in the deeper positions, Wilson becoming an infield specialist to create an enviable reputation in the leg trap. Fielding almost as much as batting played a decisive part in their careers. Lester retired, in 1956, primarily because full-time cricket was aggravating foot discomfort. Wilson was taken on the 1954–5 tour of Australia as a batting speculation justified by certainty of fielding usefulness. He was England's 12th man in every Test match.

In 1939 Yorkshire had noted the promise of another left-handed batsman of athletic build and commendable style in the orthodox mould. He was W. Watson, called Willie in distinction from his father, who, as Billy Watson, had won international renown in Association football.

After the war the younger Watson also became a professional footballer, with professional cricket a summer occupation. Willie Watson's early cricket inspired enthusiastic prophecy. His method won approval and his calm attitude suggested qualifications to follow Maurice Leyland.

He played 15 innings in 1946 and was given a full season in

1947 when he made his first county century and reached an aggregate of 1,331. 1948 confirmed development with a higher aggregate and average but 1949 brought a set-back with mid-season loss of form and relegation—as for Wilson and Wardle—to the second team for a period.

Opposing demands of football and cricket became irreconcilable in 1950 when Watson was invited to join the World Cup team visiting South America. He did not appear in Yorkshire cricket until August, but he returned to such effect that by the end of the season he had made three centuries and devised an average of 70 over 11 championship innings.

Watson was never again sent to the Yorkshire second team to find form and he became an England cricketer to record centuries against Australia and West Indies, but he was not seen as a dominating figure on either county or Test-match fields. In football and cricket he was clearly of the best material but an urge to be first among the foremost was perhaps outside his ambition.

Yorkshire's search for bowlers remained widespread through the first five seasons after the war. Smailes retired in 1948 and after 1949 Ellis Robinson was allowed to join Somerset under special registration, these departures completing the scope for replacements in every type of bowling.

Yorkshire's traditional standards were, of course, hard to meet. Several of the players brought forward and discarded made careers with other counties; Coxon and Wardle, who stayed to carry the main burden of work, mingling disappointments with satisfactions in their performances.

Both were impressively industrious. Coxon overcame the handicaps of an erratic run-up and angular action to bowl willingly and stoutheartedly through long spells, but as a bowler he was always nearer the artisan than the artist. Dominating bowling returns one wicket for every five or six overs through a season or a career. One wicket taken in, say, every ten overs means that time alone would prohibit many victories in three-day cricket.

Wardle enjoyed natural advantages as a bowler. His left-arm action was smooth, with a long swing beginning from behind the back as in the action of Blythe and Woolley, and he had strength of legs for stamina and strength of fingers for spinning the ball.

He kept his place and won his cap in 1947 when he was brought in during Booth's illness and he was rapidly elevated to international status with selection for the M.C.C. tour of West Indies in early 1948. His limitations were apparent and all the more aggravating because they were illogical and he was perhaps unfortunate in not finding more competition for the leadership of his type. His concentration did not need to be channelled as it should have been because county spin bowling of the period was notably weak and Wardle sometimes shocked the purists by deficiencies in control of length and direction uncharacteristic of the classic slow left-hander.

For all his shortcomings Wardle was an important element in the construction that began to take shape in 1949 when first place in the championship was shared with Middlesex. The outcome of that season was a relief because until mid-August Yorkshire had been unimpressive, particularly in their bowling and fielding, and the chance of equality in the championship came only because Middlesex made a weak finish to their own programme.

Yorkshire, meeting Hampshire, Derbyshire, Warwickshire, Kent, Gloucestershire and Glamorgan in travels from end to end of the championship territory, won all their last matches. They won them in accumulating excitement and with some debt to fortune, but with a commendable show of determination.

Against Hampshire at Hull rain in the night came conveniently for Yorkshire and an appropriately enterprising 59 by Lester gave time for the second disposal of Hampshire with 106 runs to spare. At Bradford Derbyshire were completely outplayed until teatime on the second day, being dismissed for 94 and then fielding to Yorkshire's declaration of 401 for four wickets.

The pitch was not at fault. Yorkshire, with their fast bowler Whitehead injured, could find no second profit in the new ball and Derbyshire batted on and on, rejoicing in 55 from

Smith, 95 from Elliott, 74 from Revill and above all 219 from Eggar. Coxon had bowled 51 overs, Wardle 81 and Close 44 by the time Derbyshire's innings ended at 491, leaving little more than an hour and a half for 185 to be attempted.

Attempt was made; attempt was successful, Watson and Coxon scoring the last 80 runs in half an hour.

At Scarborough, where Watson and Lester made centuries, Yorkshire were not so pressed for time in defeating Warwickshire by an innings and 68 runs, but the match continued far enough into the third day to compel a wearisome night journey to the next fixture in Kent.

The match was at Dover but the only hotel accommodation available was in Folkestone. Travelling from London on the milk and newspaper train the team turned out on the Folkestone platform at four o'clock in the morning to face complete darkness at the station entrance. No taxis were available.

The ticket-collector, asked for directions to the hotel, pointed into the blackness of the deserted station approach. 'Turn left,' he said, 'and then right and left again. After about ten minutes' walk you will come to the square and then anybody will tell you where the hotel is.' 'Anybody' at 4 a.m. seemed optimistic.

Perhaps excusably Yorkshire made hard work of winning at Dover and Kent could not be prevented from scoring 268 in the fourth innings to delay the beginning of another long journey to Huddersfield.

By this time Yorkshire were within sight of the championship. They could be outright winners if Middlesex dropped any points and they could share honours with two victories if Middlesex defeated Derbyshire at Lord's, as they did.

Yorkshire won at Huddersfield, but again without showing complete authority. They established advantage by dismissing Gloucestershire for 77, but Goddard's bowling and determined second-innings batting changed the prospect and Yorkshire lost seven wickets in making the 130 runs they finally required. They were pursuing success rather than commanding it.

Glamorgan took them to Newport for the last championship fixture, Yorkshire knowing that only outright victory would serve their remaining purpose. After a painstaking opening stand of 124 by Hutton and Lowson Yorkshire were all out for another 100 runs, but Glamorgan were an unstable batting side and by the end of the second day the match was over and Yorkshire were joint champions—breathlessly and with an element of thankful relief in their satisfaction.

24

Talent and turbulence

Yorkshire's entry into the 1950s was made with a feeling that a team of talent was being assembled though the probability of delays and disappointments were recognised. Fulfilment matched anticipation.

For a decade the side was never without talent, some of it at the highest level. In the 1950s ten Yorkshire players were awarded an England cap and two were England captains. Yorkshire were represented at one time or another by leaders of the national averages and players of world-wide reputation. Only twice, in 1953 and 1958, were they of minor significance in the championship and no season began without rational backing for the conventional expressions of optimism.

Yet from 1950 to 1958 Yorkshire never finished first in the table. In this they shared the experience of 16 other counties over seven successive seasons, for the decade was almost the monopoly of Surrey, but Yorkshire had no sympathy to spare for fellow-sufferers. They were regretful of their own failure to rise from the level of the good to the great. Not for half a century had nine years been allowed to pass without Yorkshire putting a championship in their pocket.

Yorkshire's failure was essentially an inability to take the last step, to crystallise individual talent, to create harmony from the varied instruments at their disposal. They came third in the championship in 1950, second in 1951 and 1952, second again in 1954 and 1955 and they were third in 1957.

They were slow to find a winning path in 1950, losing to both M.C.C. and Oxford University in the opening fixtures, losing to West Indies at Bradford and having to wait until late May before a victory over Sussex gave them a taste of satisfaction.

The sum of satisfaction was 14 victories in 24 championship games; the aggravation was inability, on two or three occasions, to grasp victories that were within reach. A catch missed, an inaccurate over bowled, a wicket thrown away hurt Yorkshire pride.

Of the three young players, Close, Lowson and Trueman, brought in during 1949 only Lowson had chance to develop. He responded with an aggregate exceeding 2,000 runs in all matches. Trueman's potentiality was noted by invitation to the Test trial at Bradford, but at the age of 19 a full season of fast bowling was mercifully prohibited and Close was limited to one championship match because he had been called to National Service.

Close gained little cricketing benefit from his military experiences. He played frequently enough but not in the atmosphere of professional application desirable at the formative stage of his career. In 1949 he was compelled to attempt too much; in 1950 his ambitions and cricketing education were left in cold storage.

In his first Yorkshire season, undertaken at the age of 18, he was hurried into the record books. He played for England, in the Manchester Test against New Zealand, and he was kept in the Yorkshire side, despite clear evidence of physical strain and declining form, to achieve completion of 1,000 runs and 100 wickets.

In 1950 he took Whitsuntide leave to join Yorkshire at Sheffield for the Lancashire match. On the last afternoon he was sharing with Yardley a partnership that gave hope of a Yorkshire victory when he slipped, fell and was run out because of inadequately studded boots. Yorkshire lost the match by 14 runs.

Later in the year Close was brought back into public controversy through being selected for the M.C.C. tour of Australia, led by F. R. Brown. Strong objections were voiced against the creation of privilege for one National Serviceman and against the inclusion of a young player currently outside the first-class ranks. Close was tossed into a stormy sea and when the waves began to envelop him nobody spread oil on the turbulent waters. His cricket on the tour was a spectacular disappointment and he experienced a bitter loneliness.

Close's absence from the county field in 1950 left Yorkshire without off-spin bowling and they sought compensation in the form, unusual to traditional thinking, of a leg-break bowler.

Yorkshire cricket, at club and county level, has never contained much distinguished leg-break bowling because conditions have offered little scope for it. By the nature of its presentation the leg-break tends to be expensive; it is more effective on the dry and broken turning pitch than on the soft and sticky; its challenge, to the right-handed majority of batsmen, can be contrived by the slow left-hander. Leg-break bowling is outside the nature of Yorkshire cricket.

In 1950 the county took E. Leadbeater from the second team and gave him a full season in first-class company. Leadbeater offered leg-breaks in the orthodox form, that is to say slow in pace and high-flighted, and 1950, being a wet summer, was not best suited to his method but he took 87 wickets to earn his keep. He was sufficiently impressive to be sent to India in the winter of 1951-2 as replacement for Derbyshire's A. E. G. Rhodes and there he played in two Test matches to reach the peak of his career. He was not re-engaged by Yorkshire after 1952.

With Leadbeater in the M.C.C. side touring India was Yorkshire's wicketkeeper D. V. Brennan, who had joined the county team in 1947. Early crudities of inexperience could not disguise an exceptional talent and by 1949 he was challenging Godfrey Evans in a Test trial at Edgbaston.

The challenge was noted and accepted. To Brennan's brilliance in a leg-side stumping Evans responded with equal magic and not until 1951 could Brennan claim an England cap, with two appearances against South Africa. Brennan played his cricket as an amateur and retired, in 1953, at the age of 33 through overriding business and personal concerns.

In 1951 his wicketkeeping problems were increased by Yorkshire's discovery of Appleyard. Discovery is justifiable term in general application because although Appleyard had played in three first-team matches in 1950 it was not until the beginning of the next season that the extent of treasure-trove was fully appreciated. In one year 'Bob' Appleyard stepped into the ranks of great bowlers.

Appleyard was a bowler's bowler. The casual observer noted results without being attracted by methods. Appleyard bowled, right-handed, at medium pace with no striking mannerisms of run-up or delivery. He was inconspicuous in that he rarely invited comment on an over of untidy length and direction. He was not obviously beating batsmen by pace or by sharp spin or by the hypnotism of swing. Pulling off his sweater, he did not rouse excitement of anticipation. Dismissed batsmen seemed to have been at fault rather than left in helplessness.

Appleyard's hidden virtues were revealed in performances. 200 wickets in his first full season expressed off-spin, inswing, variation of pace, consistent accuracy and awkward bounce of the ball derived from Appleyard's height and high action. He was never a self-satisfied bowler, content with what he was doing and could do. The spring of 1952 found him teaching himself control of the leg-cutter. His first overs in any match were given to search for the pace likely to extract most response from the condition of the pitch. He never cared to bowl at a standard below the best of which he was capable.

Appleyard's 200 wickets in 1951 could not bring Yorkshire to the position of champion county. They took second place to Warwickshire and again were not unjustly stationed because bowling, batting and fielding could not command the decisive authority at the appropriate hour. They were beaten only three times but 11 of the 28 championship fixtures were left drawn.

Yorkshire were second again in 1952 and perhaps more satisfactorily because they played nearer to their talents. Circumstances, not loss of form, imposed bowling limitations.

Appleyard played in only one match before he was taken so seriously ill that he had to spend months in hospital. Trueman was England's fast bowler but could play in few matches for his county because his turn for National Service had come. Yorkshire were a bowling side of improvisation, heavily dependent on the stamina of Wardle who took 169 wickets and on the returned Close who reached his 100 wickets in variation between medium-pace and slow off-spin. Close was also one of the seven batsmen to exceed 1,000 runs.

Maintaining a championship challenge with such limited bowling was an improbability and under additional stress in 1953 Yorkshire tumbled down the table to finish in 13th place, the lowest they had ever occupied in the 20th century.

Appleyard was still in hospital, Trueman was still in the Royal Air Force, and Close, nursing a football injury, played two innings and bowled 45 overs in the whole season. Only six matches were won and the consolation of the Yorkshire year was a Yorkshire contribution to the recovery of the Ashes from Australia. Hutton was England's captain through the series, Watson played in three Tests, Wardle in two and Trueman in one. Yorkshire hid their county face in embarrassment but claimed a share of reflected glory from England's accomplishment.

In 1954 and 1955 Yorkshire were better but not best. Surrey continued as county champions, Yorkshire taking second place without any justifiable feeling that they should have been first. They remained an agglomeration of individual talent, mainly just below greatness, lacking the element of fusion that makes an impressive team.

Appleyard and Close were back in the field in 1954, Appleyard to lead the bowling and Close to indicate that batting rather than bowling would be his future strength. Trueman, now 23 years old, had acquired a man's physique for fast bowling that questioned the courage as well as the technique of opposing batsmen. Wardle, less concerned in being a bowler for all purposes, contributed appropriate performances with nine for 48—and 16 wickets in the whole match—against Sussex at Hull and nine for 25 against Lancashire at Old Trafford.

Wardle was bowling when the match with Leicestershire at Huddersfield came to the climax that provided a new entry for Yorkshire's records. The game had changed character after first innings in which Yorkshire declared at 351 for four wickets and Leicestershire made 328. Yorkshire were put out for 113 through Spencer's pace and swing and Leicestershire's effort to score 137 carried the match to the last over of the extra-half-hour. Nine wickets were down and the total was 136 when the sixth ball of the over was delivered.

Spencer played with appropriate discretion and ran with the stroke but the ball went almost straight down the pitch for Wardle to pick up, turn and throw down the bowler's wicket to end the match as a tie.

Appleyard was top of the bowling averages again in 1955 but his was a shortened season through injury, and Hutton, in constant disability because of a strained and painful back, played only 18 innings for Yorkshire and none at all for England in the Tests against South Africa. It was his last season, as it was the last season for N. W. D. Yardley, who resigned the captaincy after holding it for eight years.

25

Philosophies at variance

Yardley and Hutton could offer acceptable public reasons for their retirement from first-class cricket without emphasising an underlying cause. They left the game partly, at least, because the playing routine was losing its attraction.

Yardley had passed through the whole range of experience. He had been university cricketer, county cricketer and Test-match cricketer, gaining selection at each level on his playing merits. He had toured South Africa and Australia and had been invited to tour even more extensively. He had captained Cambridge, Yorkshire and England. He had served as Chairman of the England selection committee.

He played in 20 Test matches and earned his keep with a batting average of 25, reliable fielding and change bowling that brought him Bradman's wicket three times, twice in one match. For Yorkshire he scored 11,632 runs, in manner invariably both attractive and appropriate to the occasion. Two of his 17 county centuries, made in successive innings in 1950, illustrated his talents at their peak. On the third day of their match with Somerset at Taunton Yorkshire were set to make 225 to win in 130 minutes and Yardley, going in first, hit 18 boundaries to be not out 120 when Yorkshire took the match.

Next day, at Old Trafford, Yorkshire met for the first time a slim young bowler named Statham, who shocked them by bowling Lowson for 0, Lester for 0 and having Watson caught in the slips for 0. Yardley came to the crease when the total was 13 for four wickets, shine still on the ball, freshness still in the air of the August morning and Lancashire flourishing a giant's challenge in their jubilation. With scarcely a mis-hit Yardley stayed for four hours to make 119 in Yorkshire's all-out score of 226.

As a captain of Cambridge University, of Yorkshire and of

England Yardley could do no more than weave a logical, orthodox, pattern from the material at his disposal. When the material was inadequate he could not devise success and he did not expect it to fall to him through a disproportionate share of good fortune. Yardley recognised merit as the groundwork of achievement and all his character, all his training, led him to accept failure or success with equal grace and equanimity.

His philosophy of cricket never changed. In his view the game should be played earnestly, sensibly and with unfailing goodwill. He assumed the same outlook in those with whom he played. If they fell below his standard he was disappointed, but not censorious.

He gave all others credit for appreciating his own approach and he was tolerant of shortcomings. In his captaincy he was forgiving rather than forceful and he never allowed a personal inclination to obscure a cricketing judgement. A player under his leadership said of him, 'He is too nice a chap to be the captain we need.'

Yardley could not have failed to become aware of the changing currents in the cricket of the 1950s. In his formative period first-class cricket was an end in itself, a life-work for the professional, a treasured interlude and experience for the amateur. In the 1950s a subtle change of emphasis became evident in all sport at high level and cricket suffered the infection, mildly at least.

Success was edged away from being its own satisfaction. It came to be viewed with an eye on its consequences, those consequences measured carefully in commercial terms. The appeal of a cricketing career involved increasing concern for the material rewards. Invitations to play brought demands for 'caps' or contracts. County effort was related, consciously or subconsciously, to its effect on publicity for Test-selection purposes. Tests and tours were valued in proportion to off-the-field perquisities obtainable from them.

Almost imperceptibly at first, some of the play became conditioned by some of the extrinsic factors involved. With money at stake and known to be at stake for specified performances a dropped catch or a running misjudgement assumed a signi-

Brian Close, Yorkshire's present captain, who played for England at the age of 18 and became England's captain at 35

John Hampshire, who scored a century in his first Test match

A spectator's view of Headingley during the Test match between England and the West Indies in 1963

Phil Sharpe, Yorkshire's opening bat and brilliant slip fielder.

The Yorkshire team in 1967. Back row, from left to right—E. Lester (scorer), P. Sharpe, G. Boycott, D. Wilson, P. Stringer, A. Nicholson, D. Padgett, J. Hampshire and G. Alcock (masseur). Front row left to right, J. Binks, F. Trueman, D. B. Close (captain), R. Illingworth and K. Taylor

Ray Illingworth, England and Leicestershire captain, who left Yorkshire after dissatisfaction over terms with the county.

ficance beyond the course of a match. Prominence through misbehaviour could be more profitable than conscientious obscurity. County cricket opened the way to the artifically stimulated glamour of Test cricket and Test cricket led to commercial careers outside cricket. Cricket was coming to be used by cricketers as a means to an end beyond cricket.

In such an atmosphere the cricket field and the dressing-room began to lose attraction or to gain attraction, according to viewpoint. Extension of television and a redirection of much cricket writing towards the cult of personality helped to shift the focus of loyalties from the corporate to the individual. The prevailing national philosophy crudely summarised in 'I'm all right, Jack . . .' infected cricket.

In this period came an explosion of self-interests exemplified in the sale of names and faces for the advertisement of commercial products having no connection with cricket. In this period came the extension of the 'ghosted' book and newspaper article from technical subjects to gossip and concoction of controversy. In this period came the translation of Test matches from games of cricket to concerns of national prestige. Any series must ostensibly be rated the equal of all others and therefore given the same terms of contest; five days for all and every match 'the greatest'.

Emphasis on the individual, glorification of the Test in tinsel trappings and diversification of personal interests all tended to detract from the appeal of county cricket in its day-to-day existence. Some players, no doubt unwittingly, began to think and talk about 'my' performance as distinct from 'our' performance and its consequences. Other players tended to resent egotism; foolish words were spoken and written for publication and harsh ones occasionally passed on the field and in the dressing-rooms. The eventual outcome in Yorkshire was dramatic.

Leonard Hutton left first-class cricket with a feeling of relief more than of regret. He had completed an exhausting journey.

In 1934, as a shy youth, he had been observed by companions in a smile and a chuckle irrelevant to the current conversation.

'What are you laughing at, Len?' he was asked.

'Me—playing for Yorkshire,' came the slow reply. Playing

cricket, and for Yorkshire, merged dreams and reality for the adolescent Hutton. His bliss was batting and batting in the highest company he could conceive was his very heaven.

The political involvements of cricketing prominence scarcely touched him until after the Second World War. Through the bewildering commercial experiences that followed his record Test score of 364 he remained a cricketer absorbed in cricket. Delight in play shone from his batsmanship in South Africa in 1938–9 and in the English summer of 1939. He was enjoying the sweets of greatness in the company of the great as he was never to enjoy them again, for in post-war cricket his greatness brought the responsibilities and reactions of comparative isolation.

In the 1950s enormous pressures of reputation descended on Hutton. He was so incomparably ahead of all other Yorkshire batsmen in technique and experience that he was scarcely ever able to play a carefree innings. He found himself batting with success assumed as a routine accomplishment and failure exaggerated in significance.

He found also that he was not allowed to bat merely as No. 1 in the order but was regarded as private enemy No. 1 by all opposing teams. In Test matches he was forced into grim self-preservation by the grim concentration of attack devoted to him.

Perhaps Hutton could have come to relish this form of compliment had it not also been paid to him by members of his own teams. Yorkshire and England tended to rely too complacently on Hutton's manifest acceptance of responsibility. Supporting players were inclined to use him as a prop and stay more than as an inspiration. Yorkshire batsmen disappointed Hutton in their failure to discuss with him the whys and wherefores of their own limitation. He could not sympathise with the same mistakes repeated.

In Hutton's Yorkshire training individual concerns were community concerns. Help in a period of struggle was as freely given as it was readily accepted, not necessarily in the form of direct instruction as from tutor to pupil, but perhaps as an oblique reference, or a demonstration, based on understanding of a common language. Hutton's hints were allusive.

The Yorkshire of Hutton's later career never seemed to acquire this unity. Hutton had learned much of his own cricket by listening and watching and thinking how suggested solutions could be applied to his own problems. He was surprised and dismayed to find the tradition being abandoned in the new cricketing world of easy self-satisfaction and, being an introvert, he tended to withdraw rather than to initiate apparently unwanted assistance.

His later international experience led him along the same lonely paths. His England captaincy, beginning in 1952, gave him more care than comfort because the policies founded on his beliefs had to be explained and practised and proved before they could become acceptable. Hutton as an England captain was always on trial, particularly in his own estimation, and he made the trial so severe that he undoubtedly cut away a quiet evening to his own playing career.

This was Yorkshire's loss and cricket's loss. Hutton in his forties, Test-match strain behind him, would have given to county cricket the reflective satisfactions that Hobbs and Woolley and Sutcliffe and Hendren were able to give through their last seasons. In Hutton's last years too much depended on the result of his innings for the beauty of his batting to be fully appreciated.

His technique was virtually without fault. There was grace and authority in his most unambitious stroke. His judgement and positioning when the ball was turning were at once a source of wonder and of comfort. He was stern critic of himself, always in search of perfection. He made an instructional film which included stroke illustrations from an actual county innings that brought him a century. 'I don't like it,' he said, on reviewing the published version. 'There is one stroke where my back-lift is not straight.' After edging a catch into the slips during a Brisbane Test he rebuked himself. 'I shouldn't have played at it,' he maintained.

For his 24,807 Yorkshire runs Hutton showed an average of 53.35. His 1949 aggregate of 2,640 is the highest recorded in Yorkshire scorebooks. He made at least one century in every season he played and he made centuries in both innings of a match on three occasions.

These are county figures but Hutton became so much an England cricketer that he almost obscured his county association. Len of local pride; Sir Leonard of national gratitude.

26

Rainy weather

After Yardley's retirement Yorkshire were captained for two seasons by W. H. H. Sutcliffe—Billy, son of Herbert.

The appointment was logical. Billy Sutcliffe, playing as an amateur, had been in first-class cricket since 1948, had made six Yorkshire centuries and had reached 1,000 runs in 1955. With every sign of careful tuition he had become a competent batsman and at the age of 29 he was not required to be a captain needing tolerance in the field.

Billy Sutcliffe was, in fact, hampered in his captaincy by the very factors that made his appointment seem so appropriate. He had been in the dressing-room, among his seniors and peers in cricket, for eight years and could, therefore, bring nothing of the slight aloofness, the detachment, desirable in leadership when discipline, or inspiration, has to be exercised.

As the son of a famous father, one still held clearly and dearly in memory and one still active and prominent in cricket administration, Billy Sutcliffe could never escape the embarrassing shadow of comparison. 'I remember your father' is an easy form of creating introduction but a stultifying approach to discussion on level terms.

Billy Sutcliffe's hardest task in cricket was to distinguish the identity of W. H. H. Sutcliffe from the identity of Herbert Sutcliffe and, almost inevitably, the attempt led Billy into exaggerations of outlook and action beyond his own natural inclinations. Before he became captain Billy was playing in a Yorkshire match that promised no more than a formality as Yorkshire's second innings. In the first innings Billy, as a middle-order batsman, had been dismissed for 0 and dressing-room proposal was made that he should be sent in first in the second innings to give him the onus of avoiding a 'pair of spectacles', a misfortune that had never befallen Herbert Sutcliffe.

Billy made stubborn protest, on grounds that he had not been required to open the first Yorkshire innings and the proposed change of order would have no relevance to the match. The intended joke was not pursued. It was no joke to Billy Sutcliffe.

Billy Sutcliffe knew when he assumed the captaincy that there were elements of disharmony in the side and the Yorkshire playing results of 1956 were discouraging. The committee report for the season, traditionally formal, expressed an opinion that 'more matches would have been won had the players played in a more determined manner on all occasions'. Losing to Surrey (twice), Lancashire, Derbyshire, Gloucestershire, Worcestershire and Essex and winning only eight matches, Yorkshire finished seventh in the championship.

Among the batsmen only Watson returned an average exceeding 40 and in a summer more helpful to bowlers than to batsmen Wardle's 105 wickets in championship fixtures cost 15 runs each and Appleyard's 94 cost 16. Watson, Wardle, Appleyard and Trueman played in Tests against Australia but none of them retained an England place through the series.

Lester played only one innings in the first team, having decided that foot weakness prohibited his continuation in cricket for six days a week. Yorkshire granted him a testimonial of £3,000 and appointed him senior professional to the second team, where his batting was an inspiration and his experience an educative influence on young players. Two seasons later he took over the second-team captaincy and later still he rejoined the first team as scorer.

Yorkshire lost another batsman at the end of the 1957 season when Watson was given release to join Leicestershire and take over the captaincy there. Watson never quite reached the cricketing heights anticipated for him at the first sight of his elegant left-handed batting, but he played impressive innings and scored heavily for both his counties and he made 23 appearances for England, touring Australia, New Zealand and West Indies.

Willie Watson was reserved in character and a suggestion of detachment, almost fatalism, was conveyed in his cricket, certainly in his Yorkshire cricket. In success or failure he was notably undemonstrative and his natural athleticism and grace of movement tended to obscure the effort and concentration he was exhibiting. His performances, at the wicket and in the field, might have won more public appreciation had they not given the appearance of being easily contrived and in some way irrelevant to the occasion, yet one of the historic rearguard actions of Test cricket was fought in his match-saving century at Lord's against the 1953 Australians.

In his last Yorkshire season Watson returned the highest aggregate in the side and scored three championship centuries, but the team remained unsettled and they were defeated four times to finish third in the championship table. Surrey, champions for the sixth successive year, defeated them by an innings at the Oval and compelled a follow-on at Bradford where the match was Wardle's benefit.

Though Yorkshire were not aware through most of the summer that Watson would be leaving and that Sutcliffe's resignation was to come they were looking to the future by giving first-team experience to products of the second team. Lowson played only 19 innings, leaving scope for the left-hander W. B. Stott, and the obviously talented K. Taylor and D. E. V. Padgett. Platt, Cowan and Ryan were given further bowling opportunities, and Ray Illingworth, with 1,193 runs and 92 wickets in all matches, was becoming a significant all-rounder.

The Yorkshire lack was not so much in talent as in unity. The team was neither grimly efficient nor gaily inconsistent. Play, by the sight and occasionally by the sound of it, was not being enjoyed and Yorkshire were made aware that they were far from the most admired or respected of opponents.

When W. H. H. Sutcliffe resigned the captaincy, the family sports-outfitting business demanding his attention, no obvious successor was waiting in the wings. The principle of professional captaincy in county teams had long been established: Berry appointed by Leicestershire, Dollery by Warwickshire and Washbrook by Lancashire, but the precedents were not helpful to Yorkshire in their considerations for 1958.

They promoted J. R. Burnet from the second team. Burnet

was essentially a club cricketer but he led the county second team to happy and successful cricket and was prepared to enter the first-class ranks at the age of 39 in circumstances that were clearly a challenge to personal authority and cricketing inexperience.

Burnet's limitations as a player were not unduly exposed in 1958 because the whole team suffered limitation in a summer of miserable weather. As many as 24 days contained no cricket at all and at Hull the turf was so saturated that inspection on the second morning brought an unprecedented but rational decision that the match should be wholly abandoned.

In brief periods of tolerable weather Yorkshire plunged into the gloom of defeat by Lancashire at Headingley where Statham took six wickets for 16 runs in Yorkshire's first innings. Compensatory success came at Sheffield where the benefit match for J. V. Wilson brought defeat to Surrey. Lock was not playing, Laker was injured during the game and could not bowl after the first day and an innings of 104 by Taylor established the advantage Yorkshire preserved to the end.

By mid-season Yorkshire were clearly going to win no championship distinction. The batting, harassed by the weather, contained little more encouragement than good form shown by Stott and promise shown by P. J. Sharpe in his first season. The bowling was disturbed by injuries to Appleyard and Cowan and the consequent improvisations were offering hope rather than promise.

During the Somerset match at Sheffield in late July the Yorkshire Secretary announced, without elaboration, that 'The Yorkshire County Cricket Club have informed J. H. Wardle that they will not be calling on his services after the end of the season.'

Wardle, at this time 35 years old, was probably at the height of his bowling powers. He had not played in the 1958 Tests against New Zealand but he had already taken 102 wickets in 28 appearances for England, he had toured Australia, South Africa and West Indies and he had been invited to join the M.C.C. tour of Australia in 1958-9 under the captaincy of

P. B. H. May. Yorkshire's laconic announcement was high explosive awaiting detonation.

From Sheffield Yorkshire went to Old Trafford for the Bank Holiday match, Wardle due to play and his name, inevitably, in every cricket conversation. The start of the game was delayed by rain, but Old Trafford was not left without excitement. The Yorkshire captain issued a statement for publication saying:

'J. H. Wardle has requested that he stand down from the match because of comments he intends to make about his colleagues in a newspaper article to be published while the match is in progress. He has been given permission to stand down and has left the ground.'

Newspaper articles duly appeared, commissioned by the *Daily Mail*, in which Wardle proffered unflattering comment on Yorkshire players, the Yorkshire captain, the Yorkshire committee and the Yorkshire coaches. After the publication of the articles the M.C.C. Secretary announced that the M.C.C. Committee would consider a situation no longer domestic to Yorkshire at their next meeting, which had been called for August 19th.

Yorkshire's committee met earlier, on August 11th, and expressed themselves:

'Yorkshire C.C.C. regret the unpleasant publicity given to their decision to dispense with the services of J. H. Wardle after the present season. In past years Wardle has been warned on several occasions that his general behaviour in the field and in the dressing-room has left much to be desired. As no improvement was shown this year the decision to dispense with his services was made, as it was unanimously considered that it was essential to have discipline and a happy and loyal team before any lasting improvement could be expected in the play of the Yorkshire XI.'

The statement went on to say that as Wardle had broken his contract with the county club by publishing comment without permission the committee were terminating his engagement forthwith. The committee put on record their 'high regard for Mr. J. R. Burnet and his predecessors in captaincy, for the loyalty and restraint shown by players in trying circumstances and for the valued work of former players acting as coaches'.

Wardle was invited to Lord's for interview by M.C.C. committee representatives who subsequently informed him that the invitation to tour Australia had been withdrawn on grounds that the newspaper articles had done grave disservice to the game.

Wardle played no more first-class cricket. He became a league professional and later appeared for Cambridgeshire—once against Yorkshire's first team in a Gillette Cup fixture. In his first-class career he took 1,842 wickets as a slow left-arm bowler, mainly of orthodox spin, though he also had command of the 'chinaman', which is the left-hander's delivery with a leg-break action.

Wardle's powers of spin, in any form, were exceptional and he had the physical resources to permit long spells of bowling. His most impressive performances were, indeed, on occasions when pitch and circumstances were against him, for too frequently when he should have been complete master he fell into disappointing inaccuracy of length and direction. He was more inclined to thrive on success than to rise to challenge and an urge towards the spectacular tended to obscure an appreciation for team needs.

In his batting, particularly, juvenile adulation was frequently allowed to influence judgement and though he played many exciting innings his ability was never fully developed. Among contemporary players his technical skill was not questioned. He could spin the ball, in any manner, as effectively as any bowler of his time; he could bat well enough to have become an accepted allrounder; his fielding was agile and co-ordinated. It was in his approach that the final step to renown could not be taken.

27

Unexpected outcome

Towards the end of April net practices the Yorkshire committee customarily entertain the players to lunch, expressing hopes and anticipations for the coming season. In 1959 the Chairman of the cricket sub-committee, A. B. Sellers, indicated that a year or two of team-building lay ahead for Yorkshire and immediate championship success was not expected. In tactful response, Burnet, the reappointed captain, suggested to his team that they should 'commit the unforgivable' and prove the Chairman wrong.

The outlook was encouraging principally in the clearance of dressing-room atmosphere. Wardle's bowling was beyond immediate replacement and Appleyard and Lowson were gone, Appleyard suffered shoulder injury in addition to uncertainty of general health, Lowson resigned to lesser cricket because of the onset of varicose veins. Trueman had toured Australia during the winter and though the experience had not been particularly strenuous or successful for him eighteen months of fast bowling tests any stamina.

No other Yorkshire bowler compared with Trueman in pace and liveliness, but R. K. Platt brought disconcerting inswing with the new ball and took 82 wickets in the championship with nine in the Bradford match against Sussex as an outstanding performance. In a summer of exceptionally fine weather slow bowlers were compelled to wait for their successes and to pay for them and though Illingworth was able to reach 100 wickets and 1,000 runs in all matches Yorkshire's bowling, with D. Wilson as the slow left-hander, usually left the batting with much to accomplish.

Variable form and fortune marked the early part of the programme in which three matches were won, two lost and three left drawn. Yorkshire looked, as they were expected to look, an average side seeking to channel and consolidate individual virtues. They were defeated by M.C.C. at Lord's because they could not raise 136 runs in the last innings against Statham's speed and Greenhough's spin and they were defeated by Lancashire at Old Trafford—for the first time in 32 years—because they began each innings badly.

They defeated Oxford University without altogether outclassing them, they defeated Nottinghamshire's shaky batting side at Middlesbrough with help from the toss, and they defeated Glamorgan at Bradford where a second-team batsman, H. D. Bird, was brought in and scored 181 not out.

By the end of May the characteristics of the side had been established, with Trueman seen as the principal bowling force, Stott and Taylor associated in first-wicket partnership and Padgett indicated as the Yorkshire batsman of the year. His first 13 innings included three centuries and gave an average of 71.

Three successive victories towards the end of June carried the side to the top of the championship table, but individual form, particularly in the batting, was too variable for the position to be held continuously. Taylor, his enterprising batting augmented by brilliant fielding in the covers, played twice for England against India but his innings were unconvincing and he was dropped and for Yorkshire he was inconsistent.

J. V. Wilson, the senior professional, lost form so completely that he played in only 15 championship matches and Sharpe was also required to seek reassurance in the second team for a period.

Yorkshire's limitations were twice exposed by Surrey. At the Oval, where low scoring rather than high had become customary, Surrey's first innings of 277 left Yorkshire always under pressure. Dramatic success by Trueman and Platt on the second evening when Surrey were dismissed for 87 offered Yorkshire a whole day in which to attempt 220 runs, but from 102 when the fourth wicket fell the final innings could limp no further than 133.

At Bradford, in July, Surrey again batted first, though they gained little benefit because after they had lost three wickets for 15 runs to the new ball and made recovery through May's splendid batting rain turned the conditions to Illingworth's liking. Yorkshire were always in batting difficulty against Loader's lively bowling. Their total was 91 in the first innings and, needing 222 to win, they had lost five second-innings wickets for 78 before Taylor and Trueman made a consolatory challenge to keep the margin of defeat down to 48 runs.

In early August Surrey's hold on the championship they had held for seven years began to show sign of weakening. Their outstanding batsman, Peter May, had been lost to them through illness; J. H. Edrich, in wonderful form, suffered a broken finger at Bradford; the dry summer imposed a strain on their bowling resources.

Yorkshire, Warwickshire and Gloucestershire all stayed near enough to Surrey to bring rare excitement to the closing stages of the championship, the lead changing hands almost match by match through a sun-blessed August.

Yorkshire stayed in competition against probability. At Scarborough they were dismissed for 84 in the first innings by Middlesex yet scored 225 in the second innings to win by four wickets. At Headingley they played pickpocket when Kent, batting through the first day and into the second, appeared, to hold secure advantage on the third morning. There, 134 behind and with five first-innings wickets standing, Yorkshire declared. Close enjoyed a bowling triumph, taking eight wickets for 41 runs, and Yorkshire found themselves with 224 to make in three hours. They won with two wickets and two minutes to spare.

Still under inspiration they went to Lord's and outplayed Middlesex, though the 81 runs they needed in the last innings cost them four wickets. After Lord's they had engagements at Bath and Bristol, requiring substitutes for Trueman and Illingworth, who were selected for the Oval Test. Somerset were just too much for them, winning by 16 runs after setting Yorkshire to score 255 in the last three hours and a quarter.

From a championship point of view this defeat was not as

costly as it might have been because Surrey's simultaneous match with Leicestershire was left drawn, but at Bristol Yorkshire's only distinction was to achieve the lowest total of the county season.

After Gloucestershire had batted first to declare at 294 for eight wickets Yorkshire were dismissed in an hour and a quarter on the second morning for 35 runs. In a hot and humid night the covered pitch had 'sweated' to leave ideal conditions for the swing bowlers and Smith and Brown completed Yorkshire's rout in 22 overs, Brown taking seven wickets for 11 runs.

Bolus, going in at No. 5, scored 12 not out; nobody following him to the crease made a run. In the whole innings two batsmen were caught at the wicket, two were lbw and six were bowled. Bolus was shrewdly, or despairingly, commanded to open the second innings and he stayed for four hours to score 91, but early on the third morning the match ended without need for Gloucestershire to bat a second time.

Surrey, whose programme led them to follow Yorkshire to Bath and to Gloucestershire (though they went to Gloucester, not Bristol), defeated Somerset as Yorkshire were losing at Bristol and in the next match they defeated Gloucestershire. Yorkshire, with Trueman and Illingworth back to strengthen the bowling, forced an early advantage at Worcester, augmented it as Stott carried his bat through an innings of 262 with his 144 not out and then lost control for an agonising period.

Worcestershire, 142 behind on first innings, reached 274 before they lost the fourth wicket of their second innings. Here Kenyon was caught at the wicket for 122 and Worcestershire made swift descent to 301 all out. Batting collapse was succeeded by fielding failures and missed catches helped Yorkshire to win by four wickets. They were still ahead in the championship table but they could still be overtaken.

Yorkshire went to Hove knowing that the points from an outright victory would assure them of the championship. Any other outcome would not necessarily end their hopes but would mean dependence on Surrey success or failure in two matches at the Oval, against Middlesex and Northamptonshire.

At Hove, in beautiful weather on a dry and trustworthy pitch, Sussex batted first to lose six wickets for 67 runs and recovered to 210 through a partnership of 90 between D. V. Smith and Pataudi. Yorkshire also began badly, with their fifth wicket lost at 81, but their restoration was even more substantial, Illingworth playing admirably for 122 and Birkenshaw and Wilson helping.

The Sussex second innings promised little scope for a Yorkshire victory. By one modest partnership after another a total of 311 was built and Yorkshire in the field looked far from a conquering team. If they had a consolation it was in the form of news from the Oval where Surrey were being grimly outplayed by Middlesex.

When the last Sussex wicket had been taken an hour and three-quarters remained for play at Hove and Yorkshire needed 215 runs. By the championship system of the year a draw would bring them no more points than a defeat, therefore batting policy required no discussion. The runs had to be attempted.

After the first over the total was 15. After half an hour it was 77, with Taylor and Close dismissed; Stott and Padgett put on 141 in little more than an hour, Sussex losing all control of the cricket. They bowled wide, they bowled short, they scattered fieldsmen to leave broad pathways to the boundary and ample scope for running singles and twos. The batting was superbly enterprising without being recklessly uninhibited. The out-cricket was pathetically unsophisticated. Stott scored 96 in 86 minutes; Padgett's hour brought him 79 runs. When Yorkshire reached 200, for four wickets, they had 20 minutes in hand and they had seven minutes and five wickets to spare when the winning hit was made.

Yorkshire had won the championship, romantically and literally 'off their own bats'. They went home to a memorable reception at the Scarborough Festival and there repeated their performance almost in precise detail to beat M.C.C. by scoring 260 in 25 minutes less than the two and a half hours they had been given.

The golden autumn was extended into mid-September. The

Champion County beat the Rest of England at the Oval, recovering from the indignity of follow-on to score 425 in their second innings and win by 66 runs.

Yorkshire's final batting of 1959 carried prophecy for 1960, unappreciated at the time. J. V. Wilson made his only century of the season, J. R. Burnet was bowled for 0.

28

Professional precedence

Cricket was not allowed to evade the increasing trend of sport to develop commercial aspects and some, at least, of the professional players were insistent that the game at national and county level could best serve professional ends only through direction and exploitation from the professional point of view.

Yorkshire followed the trend of the times and when Burnet resigned the captaincy they appointed J. V. Wilson, the senior among their professional players, to lead the side in 1960.

J. V. Wilson had been in first-class cricket since 1946 when he played eight innings. By 1948 he had attained a regular place in the first team, scoring his first two county centuries, winning admiration for the power in his strokes, inducing a shake of the head by exhibiting occasional crudities of method.

The power increased rather than diminished; the crudities were never entirely eliminated and were perhaps made more evident because he was a left-hander. His backlift was towards second slip and his downswing was in a wide curve. In his periods of good form the methods were immaterial because the middle of the bat met the ball; when the eye was out prospects of another run ever accruing seemed remote in the extreme.

Dependent only on technical accomplishment Wilson would have scored far fewer than the 20,539 runs he made for Yorkshire. He brought to his innings the virtues of a stout heart. He was not dismayed by his own confusion. He was prepared to struggle through discomfort to easier times and experience taught him that dark hours invariably precede a dawn.

Twice in his career he was sent to the second team to seek the form that was eluding him at first-class level and in the year before he was made captain he lost his place in mid-season, returning for the last match to score a determined 105. His

L

selection for the M.C.C. Australia tour of 1954-5 was greeted with misgiving over the quality of his batsmanship and misgiving was duly justified by results, yet Wilson was named in the team-sheet for every Test because his fielding, adaptable to any position, made him an unquestioned choice as 12th man.

As Yorkshire's captain Wilson was acceptable to the professional players on grounds of his seniority and his playing value and on the assumption that any lack of experience in authority would be compensated for by the scope for consultation with fellow-players of perhaps greater cricketing shrewdness.

In the outcome Wilson contributed no more and no less than was expected of him in leading Yorkshire to championship success in 1960. He initiated no novelty in playing tactics, lit no flame of inspiration, yet the team preserved a unity and the spirit to recover from setbacks, which included two defeats by Lancashire.

Yorkshire in 1960 were good enough to win the championship without laying any pretensions to being an outstanding side. They were defeated six times in the championship, seven times in their full programme and in eight successive mid-season fixtures they were restricted to one victory, two defeats and five draws.

The strength of the side was competent fielding, to which J. G. Binks, the wicketkeeper, contributed 97 catches, adding 11 stumpings to create a county record, and Trueman's bowling. Although he was wanted by England for all the five Test matches against South Africa Trueman took 150 wickets for Yorkshire, serving as both fast bowler and as fast-medium bowler from a shortened run. In either capacity he was the foundation of the attack, heading the averages with figures vastly superior to those of any supporting bowler.

Against Northamptonshire at Sheffield he took seven wickets in each innings, he took seven wickets in the Warwickshire second innings at Bradford and seven in each innings in the overwhelming defeat of Surrey at the Oval.

When Trueman was not in action Yorkshire were usually

compelled to wait for wickets, the slower bowlers gaining little encouragement from a summer of broken weather because the championship rules of the year insisted on pitch-protection. The slow left-hander D. Wilson paid 22 runs for each of his 72 championship wickets, taken at a rate of less than one in 12 overs, and Illingworth frequently abandoned off-spin for swing at medium pace.

Five batsmen reached 1,000 runs in all matches, but nobody averaged 40 and the batting as a whole was unconvincing because so many of the innings carried an air of improvisation. Stott and Taylor dissolved their first-wicket partnership; Close ranged from the magnificence of 198 against Surrey and 184 against Nottinghamshire to innings of depressing ineffectuality and though Padgett played in two Test matches his batsmanship showed more culture than authority.

In 1961 the flaws in Yorkshire's cricketing material were revealed more clearly and the championship was conceded to Hampshire, with Yorkshire and Middlesex maintaining pursuit to create an interest into late August. Relative merits of the three leaders were not easily assessed because of so-called 'sporting' declarations that obliterated advantage gained and because the outcome of matches between the leaders contradicted final placings.

Yorkshire drew with Hampshire at Headingley early in the season and won at Bournemouth after the championship had been decided. Hampshire lost to Middlesex at Lord's and drew with them at Portsmouth, where Middlesex were required to save the game without having any prospect of winning it. Yorkshire were twice beaten by Middlesex, who looked and proved themselves the better side in both matches.

Through May and into early June Yorkshire enjoyed almost uninterrupted success. They won seven of their first eight championship matches but as opposition strengthened their own shortcomings became more significant. In nine days they lost to Middlesex, lost to Gloucestershire and had to recover from a first innings of 84 to save a match against Surrey.

Through late July and early August they endured another unprofitable period, which included a comprehensive defeat at

Leicester, and in the away matches that ended their programme they were beaten by Kent, beaten by Middlesex and could not contrive a sight of victory in a drawn match with Warwickshire.

The season's experiences suggested that Yorkshire were without the underlying strength to withstand pressure. The faster bowling was uncomfortably dependent on Trueman's mood and accomplishment; the slow bowling was not always masterful when it should have been. The batting ranged from the vivid to the vacuous and in sum promised more than it performed.

Infirm policy no doubt contributed to playing infirmities. The team was never settled in constitution, a batting order was never established and a bowling and field-setting routine was never devised. Long before the end of the season Yorkshire looked tired and confused.

Confusion was not entirely cleared away in 1962 but it was partly hidden by success that brought the championship in a dramatic climax to the county programme. When Yorkshire came to their last match, against Glamorgan at Harrogate, they knew that only outright victory would give them a final lead in the table.

The unstable summer weather continued into September and when Yorkshire had won the toss Glamorgan were sent in to bat on a soft pitch that allowed the ball to turn unpredictably. With 10,000 spectators raised to a state of ecstasy Glamorgan were dismissed for 65, D. Wilson taking six wickets, of which two were memorable because he held catches for himself by stretching full length in dives across the wicket.

Glamorgan had no left-arm spin bowler but the medium pace of Shepherd and Wheatley and the capriciousness of the drying turf set problems beyond solution by all the Yorkshire batsmen except Taylor. To a total of 101 Taylor contributed 67, rejoicing in occasional fortune but driving superbly through the covers and wide of mid-on. In the closing 45 minutes of the entrancing day Glamorgan began their second innings and scored 13 runs without losing a wicket.

In this state of balance the game remainded until the third morning. The second day was lost entirely to rain of density varying from drizzle to downpour. By teatime half the ground was under water.

Incredibly, cricket was feasible without delay on the sunny last day. Long hours of ground-staff labour had removed the standing water from the turf and though rivulets had run beneath the covers the pitch could not have been more difficult than on the first morning. Every over was an anxiety to both teams. Yorkshire bowled always in fear of an assault that might decide the issue. Glamorgan batted in constant expectation of losing a wicket. Spectators, greater in number than even on the first day, sat in the shadow of syncope.

In the morning's play 62 runs were scored and seven wickets were taken. As much desperation was evident in Yorkshire as in Glamorgan.

For 40 minutes after lunch Yorkshire could do nothing more. Two tail-end batsmen, Ward and Evans, constructed the biggest and longest partnership of the innings and Yorkshire's primary spin bowling confessed defeat. Close was brought on.

He began with a long hop which was cut for 4; he finished with three wickets in an over and a half and Yorkshire needed 66 to win. They made them at a cost of three wickets and became champion county of the year.

The ultimate achievement was the season's satisfaction. Yorkshire became champions without dominating the championship. Seen in their better hours they looked a side as good as any among the counties; in adversity they drooped.

For J. V. Wilson the championship success represented a reward for an exhausting experience. Through the summer an imperfect sympathy had developed between captain and some players, with disciplinary action demanded, and though Wilson set an impeccable standard of endeavour by example there were times when he was clearly not representing a source of inspiration.

P. J. Sharpe more than any other individual had reason to enjoy 1962. His aggregate of funs exceeded 2,000, he knew no prolonged period of failure and to successful batting he added brilliant slip fielding that brought him 71 catches. Illingworth bowled industriously for his 100 wickets and found splendid batting form in the later matches to exceed 1,000 runs. Binks joined David Hunter and W. R. Allen as a wicketkeeper contributing to six wickets in an innings and though he was still without an England cap his capacity was widely recognised.

At the end of 1962 Yorkshire had no reason to look into their future with despondency but they knew they would need a new captain and reinforcement in both batting and bowling.

29

Captaincy for Close

Yorkshire's captain for 1963 was, predictably, D. B. Close. He inherited the office as senior among the playing professionals, as a cricketer who had already touched the highest level of the game without being able to climb on to that elevated platform and as a candidate whose rejection would undoubtedly have opened a door to controversy within the county. By appointing J. V. Wilson in 1960 Yorkshire virtually committed themselves to appoint D. B. Close in 1963.

In 13 years of first-class cricket Brian Close had undergone bewildering experiences. In his first season of 1949 he had been hurried into his county cap because England had chosen him for a Test match and he had been harried beyond his physical resources to the distinction of 1,000 and 100 wickets.

Controversy followed him into his period of compulsory National Service because he was extracted from the obscurity to tour Australia where he was unmercifully exposed to the consequences of spectacular success and spectacular failure. On return to a county-cricket career Close remained disinclined to accept the limitations of farsighted advice and felt that the fates rather than philosophical logic were against him when his cricket was hindered by injury deriving from professional football.

Only slowly and intermittently could he find his way back to international cricket and again, in 1961, the spectacular was in the form of failure that made newspaper headlines and raised discussion throughout the world of sport.

When Close became captain of Yorkshire he was 32 years old, saddled with a public reputation for irresponsibility, seen as a gifted batsman and a bowler of modest but uncrystallised talent and recognised within the Yorkshire team as a tactician whose views had sometimes received less than due appreciation in the period of Wilson's captaincy.

Close himself expressed no doubts of his qualifications for leadership and found in his appointment a renewed zest for his personal participation in cricket. He devoted himself to the business of Yorkshire captaincy and he showed a clear understanding of the problems of 1963. They involved a harmonising of older and younger players, a calculation of talents to capitalise strengths and cloak weaknesses and the infusion of spirit.

The immediate outcome was success for Yorkshire, who retained the championship, success for Close, whose form took him back into the England team against West Indies to play the innings of the year at Lord's, and success in the creation of positive approach in the county side.

Yorkshire could not be a settled side because of injuries and Test-match calls and Binks alone played in all the 28 championship fixtures, which brought three defeats but enough outright victories, 13, to hold off the challengers. Principal contributions came from established players, shrewdly utilised, but outstanding features of the season were batting successes of G. Boycott and bowling accomplishments of A. G. Nicholson.

Boycott came into the side after Padgett had been injured and with an impressive 145 against Lancashire at Sheffield indicated a future of determined batsmanship that brought another century against Lancashire in August, a century against Leicestershire at Scarborough and a season's average 11 runs higher than that of any other Yorkshire player. Nicholson, reinforcing the faster bowling, took 69 wickets in the year, and indicated to batsmen as well as to more distant observers a quality unanticipated from a rather unconvincing action.

He and all other supporting bowlers had to bear comparison with Trueman who took 76 wickets in the championship, 34 in Tests and 129 in all matches. By this time firmly in the category of senior cricketers Trueman was well aware of his position and its implied privileges and both his energies and his resolve had to be nurtured. Under inspiration he was irrepressible, taking five wickets in each innings when Yorkshire defeated West Indies at Middlesbrough, eight for 45 against

Gloucestershire at Bradford and making memorable the Edgbaston Test with a match return of 12 for 119.

For personal delight in another sphere of activity he also made two centuries, one against Northamptonshire which was timely in the context of the match and the other, entirely appropriate to the occasion, in the Scarborough Festival where he hit six sixes and 11 fours in 67 minutes.

Close began the year in wonderful batting form, collecting 500 runs in his first nine innings and his 70 in the closing hours of the Lord's Test came into the classification of cricket heroism. Sharpe, by contrast, could scarcely put a foot right, possibly because he seemed unable to put a foot outside the popping crease, and his championship aggregate and average dropped alarmingly. Ironically, his slip fielding brought him three Test invitations and he played valuable innings at Edgbaston and the Oval.

Sharpe, Taylor, Trueman and Boycott were the Yorkshire players chosen to play for England against Australia in 1964, but only Boycott remained obviously an England choice for the future at the end of the series. Trueman was selected for the first three Tests, omitted from the fourth and recalled for the fifth in which he completed a coveted personal record, but as a fast bowler, for both England and Yorkshire, he could not evade the touch of time's finger.

Trueman's decline, not from skilful and purposeful and beautiful bowling but from devastating fast bowling, was no doubt accelerated by the change in 1964 to a no-ball law in which the front foot and the popping crease were criteria. Bowlers with a long run-up culminating in a long delivery stride found difficulty in revising the practices of years and in their consciousness of need for adjustment tended to lose the rhythm that is one of the factors creating great bowling.

Trueman found, as all must find who play cricket for long enough, that he was not as good as he used to be in the features that gave him greatest satisfaction. He could not dominate the early batsmen and he could not bring tail-enders to a summary dispatch.

His nature would not accept the inevitable. He who had

been a master for so long was not prepared to serve as assistant, particularly as obvious successors in superiority were difficult to name. Though Trueman was clearly not the fast bowler England and Yorkshire wanted in 1964 his advocates could reasonably ask who was any better.

Certainly, no one filled his Yorkshire purpose. Illingworth was a bowler of professional competence but dependent on helpful conditions for match-winning performances with off-breaks. D. Wilson had not attained the bowling maturity of which his captain, among others, believed him capable. Nicholson, routing Lancashire at Headingley in the best of several notable performances, thrived on success without suggesting the probability of eventual advance to unequivocal greatness.

By mid-season Yorkshire had become a struggling team, unsure of themselves and unlikely to retain the championship. They tended to lose contact with each other and with their ideals and autumn was welcomed with some sense of relief as well as for a rest.

Though 1964 brought twilight to Trueman's day as a fast bowler his skill and experience within physical limitations kept him in first-class cricket for another three seasons and his retirement in 1968 was by his own decision. To the end of his career he remained a cricketer of exceptional significance in public opinion and his place among the truly great bowlers of cricket history is beyond question.

When his powers were at their peak he was an enthralling sight in action. For his greater pace he had a long, accelerating run-up ending in a wide delivery stride, 'cartwheel' swing of the arms and balanced follow-through. The excellence of his method was not only thrilling to watch but contributory to remarkable freedom from the injuries so frequently consequent on the wear and tear of fast bowling.

Trueman both bowled and behaved like a fast bowler relishing authority. He made no apology for his own strength, offered no concession to opposing weakness. If he saw sign of dislike for bumpers he bowled bumpers. He reacted sharply to all forms of stimulant, from hero-worship to disparagement, from helpful pitch to the challenge of sturdy batting. He played always in the colours of a strikingly extrovert character, well aware of his own significance. In bowling, batting and fielding he wanted the centre of the stage and he took no pains to avoid limelight off the field. He was sent home from a match by one captain, he was suspended for a period by his county committee, he brought embarrassment to authority on tours, but fortune and his own resilience invariably brought him a notable performance to eliminate public disfavour. His name on the team-sheet was an advertisement for any match.

In technique he became highly accomplished. He had much more than mere speed at his command, for he learned inswing and outswing and variation of pace and length. At reduced speed and from a shortened run he could be a fast-medium bowler of the highest class, startlingly effective as the 1961 Australians discovered at Headingley, but despite his own public resolutions he could never reconcile himself to complete abandonment of the flamboyance of fast bowling.

His figures perhaps rather overestimated his Test-match significance because he had opportunity to take many wickets against weaker countries, but his county value was certainly not overrated by his Yorkshire returns. Through many seasons his bowling alone gave Yorkshire cricket a character.

30

Success in two spheres

In 1965 Yorkshire finished fourth in the championship and drew little satisfaction from a disturbed season. Dressing-room dissension, discouraging weather and poor pitches contributed to cricket as disappointing in its general appearance as in its outcome. Of the 28 championship matches only nine were won and 14 were left drawn; in the four outright defeats one new and unwanted record was established.

At Middlesbrough in May Yorkshire played Hampshire and began the match by losing their first seven wickets for 47 runs, bowlers rejoicing in an utterly untrustworthy pitch that offered high distinction for any individual innings of 50, even allowing for a catch missed here and there. Trueman scored 55 in Yorkshire's first innings total of 121; R. E. Marshall scored 51 in Hampshire's 125.

In their second innings Yorkshire were all out for 23, the smallest total in their history.

The shadow of this devastation hung over them for a month and they knew no championship victory again until they won at Trent Bridge in the last days of June. In this grim period they were beaten by Glamorgan and beaten by Northamptonshire and in early July they were beaten by Surrey.

The consolation of the season was success in the Gillette Cup, the sponsored knock-out competition of one-day, overs-limit matches introduced in 1963 as a stimulant for ailing county cricket attendances.

To reach the final Yorkshire played through three rounds. They won undramatically at Leicester, won at Taunton where Trueman took six wickets for 15 runs in Somerset's dismissal for 63 and won at Edgbaston after sitting through two wet days and then taking victory with the assistance of five Warwickshire batsmen who contrived, incredibly, to be run out.

Yorkshire travelled to Lord's for the Cup Final from Scarborough, where their third day against Derbyshire had been washed away. They reached London in torrential rain and on Saturday morning were not so much surprised to find the start against Surrey delayed as to find play within contemplation.

The toss gave Surrey choice of innings but they chose unwisely in fielding. Bowlers and fieldsmen were uncertain of foothold and though the pervading dampness in the turf made early batting cautious Close changed the mood and defined the course of the day. He inspired Boycott and the second-wicket partners took 192 runs from 37 overs. Close made 79, Boycott continued to 146 and Surrey's allotted 60 overs provided Yorkshire with a total of 317 for four wickets.

The issue was decided. A Yorkshire concession of more than five runs over to a side batting in evening light after a shattering experience in the field was beyond conception. Yorkshire were not even merciful. In the ninth over Trueman took the wickets of Edrich, Smith and Barrington and the remainder of the innings was token resistance. Surrey were all out for 142.

The Gillette Cup success of 1965 was undoubtedly influential on the championship success of 1966. It created a sunnier mood in Yorkshire's players and supporters, who are never entirely in sympathy unless the team is winning, and it opened new prospects to and for Boycott in masterful batsmanship.

Boycott's figures for 1966 were not outstanding—he scored 1,854 runs for an average of 39.44—but his approach was authoritative. He looked, and was, the only Yorkshire batsman likely to be chosen for England without provoking comment and though his judgement in running between wickets was still not impeccable and his ability to count the number of balls in an over was noted with cynicism he had clearly become a cricketing presence.

In the championship programme of 1966 Boycott made four centuries, two in one match against Nottinghamshire; Close made two and no other Yorkshire batsman made even one. This reflected the season's conditions of play, for again pitches throughout the country were underprepared and new regulations compelled first innings declaration after 65 overs in certain predetermined fixtures.

Yorkshire disliked the scheme but it brought them no specific embarrassment. They won the majority of their 'limited' engagements and in their whole programme claimed 15 victories from 28 matches. By early August they were so far ahead in the table that the championship seemed assured to them, but in six matches they were beaten three times and a dramatic late challenge by Worcestershire meant that Yorkshire entered their last match, against Kent, at Harrogate, needing an outright win to be certain of the title.

The pitch was soft and the weather unsettled and Boycott's resolute 80 was the basis of Yorkshire's first innings of 210, which served for a comforting lead of 91. Comfort departed when Yorkshire fell subservient to Underwood on the second day and were all out for 109 and comfort was not restored by a third morning delay after heavy rain.

In 'another part of the forest' the scene created equal palpitation. Worcestershire had been behind on first innings against Sussex but were recovering to give themselves sight of victory that would be conclusive if Yorkshire could not win.

Yorkshire were the favoured of fortune. A drying wind blew across the Harrogate ground after groundsmen had swept away the surface water with valiant industry and afternoon play became possible. Kent, needing 201, were beyond 100 with only three wickets down when news spread from Worcester that Sussex had won. Yorkshire could afford to lose but avoided anti-climax by winning, Illingworth and Wilson bringing the Kent innings sharply to its close when the pitch turned treacherous as it dried.

The climax represented the principal satisfaction of the season. Yorkshire felt themselves rightfully champions but knew relief when the coronation was accomplished. Neither the batting nor the bowling had been consistently impressive but in fielding, at least, Yorkshire had led all the counties. They were creative.

As counter to the prevailing inswing and off-spin batsmen had devised a cautious and ugly forward stroke in which pad and bat were thrust down the wicket together and Yorkshire saw catches within reach of a short square leg or a silly point stationed a yard or two from the batsman.

The fielding enterprise was manifestly perilous. A full-blooded shot or even a mis-hit of any power could bring serious injury. Avoiding-action was impossible in the time available. The fielding function was to take catches from purely defensive strokes and to be a batting harassment by mere presence.

Close's cricketing judgement came frequently into question, his courage never. As Yorkshire's captain and with a firm belief in his own ability he not only placed himself in the 'silly' positions but ventured a yard or so nearer the bat than either custom or duty demanded. From this position he dived to take catches that would not have been catches to more discreet fielding and he also imposed on batsmen an uneasiness, a claustrophobia, that invested Yorkshire's bowling with a menace beyond the intrinsic virtues.

The Yorkshire team responded to Close's daring with admiration for that daring and with appreciation for Close's general tactics of captaincy when they were demonstrably successful. The championship of 1966 was won by leadership as much as by batting and bowling performances and before the end of the season Close's captaincy had won national recognition.

England lost the Test rubber against West Indies in the first four matches. They were beaten by an innings and in three days at Old Trafford, where M. J. K. Smith continued the captaincy he had held in the winter's tour of Australia. For the Lord's Test Cowdrey was England captain and a match containing much splendid cricket was left drawn, but at Trent Bridge and Headingley England were outplayed and heavily defeated.

The Oval Test therefore offered the England selectors scope for the comprehensive team revision increasingly demanded by public opinion—or, at least, by critical opinion, which claims to be both reflector and moulder of public opinion.

Close was made captain. The appointment was widely applauded and the outcome was dramatically successful, though the course of the cricket obscured its logic in bedazzling glamour. Close did instil a sense of purpose and initial assurance into his team; he did carry the challenge immediately to his opponents with enterprising bowling management and field-setting; he did maintain sturdy spirit through discouraging hours and he did recognise and seize the moment of advantage that decided the issue. He could have done no more by personal effort and inspiration. The rest was done for him by quirks of cricket.

England began splendidly with the fourth West Indian wicket taken at 74 and the businesslike approach was not dissipated during a stand of 122 by Kanhai and Sobers. West Indies were dismissed for 268.

Whatever control a captain may exercise cannot be extended to his team's batting except in writing out the order and requesting appropriate performance. Captaincy can influence bowling decisively, but there is little a captain or anyone else can do for the batsman taking strike. As Close could not be held responsible when England descended to 166 for seven, so he could not be given credit for the astonishing recovery to 527 all out, which included stands of 217 for the eighth wicket and 128 for the last wicket.

Where captaincy became significant and praiseworthy again was in application of pressure to consolidate the unexpected advantage. Close kept victory firmly and clearly in the mind of his team and when a supreme gesture of authority was required he was able to make it. As Sobers came in at 137 for five Close took up position at very short leg, suggesting that his fast bowler should invite a hook and, from Sobers' mistiming, was presented with gentle catch, first ball.

Close had climbed to the peak of his cricketing career.

Few careers have had the peaks and troughs so steeply sided. An early elevation to Test-match status brought the appellation of 'boy-wonder' and cricketing demands beyond the physical and mental capacity for response. Brian Close was a boy plunged into a man's harsh world; the lights were dazzling, the shadows lonely. Before his 21st birthday he had been hailed into the company of the great and dismissed into the temperamentally unstable.

For a decade Close's cricket was clouded. He played only rarely for England and he played in county cricket that gave satisfaction mainly in direct proportion to personal success or failure. He acquired cricketing knowledge, but he found little scope, or encouragement, to display cricketing wisdom. In his own play he developed a sense of fatalism that diminished his vast ability. When he was in form the imagination could not conceive a more impressive left-hand batsman and he revelled in power; out of form he was inclined to bemoan the incidence of misfortune without feeling responsibility to redirect the course of the cricketing fates.

The Yorkshire captaincy came to him by professional seniority when J. V. Wilson retired. Without it Close might never have reached fulfilment as a cricketer. It served as his step to maturity. He brought earnest endeavour to office and he spread conviction from his own convictions. He established authority and he enjoyed its exercise, coming to appreciate the disadvantages of leadership only in his second and third seasons when he discovered the difference between reactions of a winning and a losing side. Cricket was full of meaning for him and the skies of the future were clear with England restored to dignity and Yorkshire restored to the throne of county champions at the end of 1966.

31

Reprimand

The summer of 1967 brought another championship to Yorkshire, another controversy to cricket and another turn in the career of Brian Close.

As in 1966, championship success was confirmed only in the last match. Yorkshire this time needing at least first innings points from Gloucestershire at Harrogate, though in fact they won outright and so obtained a comforting margin of advantage over Kent and Leicestershire.

In the beginning Yorkshire suffered a dismal experience. The fixture list gave them five home matches in May, followed by Whitsuntide at Old Trafford. In this period no fewer than nine days were completely without cricket and three others permitted play only for an hour or two. At Headingley the match with Leicestershire was abandoned without a ball bowled and at Old Trafford prospect of play was so hopeless that players were given notice that attendance at the ground would be without point.

Only the game with Worcestershire at Hull pursued a course approaching the normal, Yorkshire winning by five wickets after stern batting by Padgett and Close and effective off-spin by Illingworth had created advantage. Outright victory was also achieved over Nottinghamshire at Bradford, but it was nominal because a result was contrived through three declarations, Nottinghamshire losing only five wickets in the match and Yorkshire being offered the last two hours to hit off 150 runs.

On this occasion Yorkshire were unimpressive in their bowling. A fortnight earlier, on the same ground, their batting was disastrous. They were dismissed for a total of 40 by Kent, for whom Graham and Sayer presented fast-medium bowling beyond the power of Trueman and Nicholson to equal.

When, at last, the sunshine came Yorkshire were able to assess their resources. They found themselves with uneven batting and with ineffective opening bowling. Trueman could not sustain speed and Nicholson, troubled by injuries and out of luck, had taken only 20 wickets by mid-June. Later in the season Nicholson began to find the edge of the bat more rewardingly but Trueman was rarely dominant and his 57 championship wickets were at an average of 22.

Bowling experiments were made. P. Stringer was introduced to first-class cricket against M.C.C. at Lord's and his lively pace brought him four wickets for 10 runs before a strained side compelled him to leave the field. In his next match he took three wickets in one over, but at Bradford he lost rhythm and subsequent injury prevented any real chance of development. A younger bowler, C. Old, played in eight championship games and took 20 wickets, but he, too, was harassed by injury and seam-bowling support in August was supplied by R. A. Hutton, who found translation from club to county standards a demanding experience.

Close captained England in the six Tests of the summer and had Illingworth with him in four of them, but Yorkshire found off-spin replacement in G. Cope who bowled to such effect that, with 40 wickets, he was placed second in the national averages and easily first in Yorkshire's championship figures.

Once the floods had subsided Yorkshire were never far from the top of the table, but five outright defeats spread through the season permitted challengers to remain in contact. Leicestershire under Lock were temporary leaders in July, but when Yorkshire went to Leicester they proclaimed themselves unequivocally the stronger force with an innings victory that represented perhaps the peak of Yorkshire performance in approach and achievement.

By early August Kent had both championship and Gillette Cup within reach. They won the Cup but lost grasp on the championship in the Canterbury Week when Yorkshire defeated them. The Trent Bridge Test took away Cowdrey, Knott and Underwood from Kent and Close and Boycott from Yorkshire, Dixon and Trueman captaining the county sides.

They played appropriate parts. Dixon taking seven wickets in Yorkshire's first innings and Trueman hitting 33 runs when Yorkshire were rather desperately in arrears. In the decisive hour Kent dropped catches and then began their second innings by losing three wickets for five runs. They were not allowed to reassert themselves.

Kent were able to stay in contention to the season's end only because Yorkshire were checked in August. Rain brought two blank days at Bradford, an historic match at Edgbaston was left drawn and Essex turned a Scarborough occasion upside down to win by nine runs after they had been far behind on first innings.

The Edgbaston draw brought repercussions that reverberated round the cricketing world. For two days, in showery weather, the game remained attractively fluctuating. Boycott and Hampshire in partnership gave Yorkshire first-morning assurance; the fall of five wickets between 108 and 115 melted it away. Wilson and Trueman gave Hampshire chance to complete a splendid century and Yorkshire reached 238.

At 201, when their fifth wicket fell, Warwickshire seemed certain of first innings points, but they won them only with their last batsmen together and were all out for 242 an hour before the close on the second day.

To this point the game had been an interesting contest in cricket, strength and weaknesses exhibited in both teams, but for the observant some straws were blowing in the wind. Yorkshire's bowling and fielding on the second morning left much to be desired and as the players went in for lunch an exasperated Close heard a derogatory remark addressed to him. Close, seeking the speaker, made a mistaken identification and any intended retaliation had to be abandoned, though Close did report the pavilion enclosure incident to the Warwickshire secretary.

On the field Yorkshire raised a point of morality towards the end of the day's play. Boycott had been excused his fielding turn because of a bruised foot and Yorkshire had benefited, legitimately enough, from the substitution of Taylor, but when Yorkshire faced an awkward 50 minutes of batting against the new ball Boycott was sent in first to exercise his particular skill and experience. Yorkshire broke no written law but they certainly pressed the concessions of custom to the limit.

The third day's weather was gloomy and showery. Yorkshire batted defensively and ineffectively and had all catches been held they would have been out by lunchtime. A seventh-wicket stand of 45 by Illingworth and Binks and a weather interruption eventually left Warwickshire needing 142 to win in 100 minutes.

In this attempt, which failed by nine runs, Warwickshire lost five wickets. Yorkshire's policy was entirely of containment. The only bowlers were Trueman with four overs, Nicholson with 11 and Hutton with nine. Light rain fell intermittently, wetting the grass and necessitating the use of towels to dry the ball. Run-saving fields were set, but Warwickshire kept victory always within possibility.

Yorkshire made no effort to disguise their delaying tactics. They walked slowly to bowling marks, to positions in the field and between overs. They were provocatively tardy in retrieving the ball from the boundary and returning it to play. Spectators grew increasingly discontented and abusive and the whole atmosphere of the game degenerated to disillusion with the basic principles of sport.

When 15 minutes remained, with 24 runs wanted from the seven wickets then standing, Yorkshire appealed against the conditions in the onset of heavier rain. Appeal was disallowed but in an even sharper shower Yorkshire ran from the field and were in the dressing-room before umpires and batsmen had reached the pavilion gate. As the rain stopped suddenly the umpires turned back to the middle.

Two more overs were bowled. In one of them, which contained two no-balls, Amiss was caught and bowled by Trueman from a mis-hit hook. For the other, which came to be the last, Hutton was called from the deep field. He conducted his preliminary routine with calculated deliberation, bowled a full toss and took a wicket. Warwickshire could stretch their effort no further.

Yorkshire's players left the field to the scorn of spectators and left Edgbaston for Scarborough with the two championship points awarded for escaping defeat. Repercussions followed them.

Statutory report from the Edgbaston umpires initiated a meeting of the Executive Committee formed by the counties—not by M.C.C. or for M.C.C. as was widely believed—and the conduct of the Warwickshire *v.* Yorkshire match was considered. Close, whose written justification of Yorkshire's tactics was in the hands of the Committee, chose to travel by road from his home to London on the morning of the meeting and because of mechanical failure in his car he was late in arriving. The meeting was delayed to ensure a personal hearing for the Yorkshire captain and at its conclusion the verdict was issued.

The Committee 'came to the unanimous decision that the Yorkshire team had used delaying tactics during the second Warwickshire innings and that these tactics constituted unfair play and were against the best interest of the game.

'Furthermore, the Committee held the captain Brian Close entirely responsible for these tactics. They have, therefore, severely censured him and this decision will be conveyed to the Yorkshire County Cricket Club.'

These findings were acknowledged and accepted by Yorkshire who announced that steps would be taken to prevent repetition of such offence and county cricket rules were subsequently amended to ensure the bowling of at least 20 overs, if necessary, in the last hour of a match.

For Close personally the reprimand carried additional concern and consequences because it was given on the eve of a Test match in which Close was the appointed captain of England and at a time when announcement of an M.C.C. team to tour West Indies was imminent. Close led England against Pakistan at the Oval without knowing the team for West Indies and whether or not it would be under his captaincy. He had been England's captain in seven successive home Tests, not entirely without adverse criticism, but successful by measure of results and clearly meaningful in approach. He was eager to lead a touring side, he was anticipating England *v.* Australia in 1968 and he was the man in possession of office.

The M.C.C. team for West Indies was announced on the day following the period allotted to the Oval Test and M. C. Cowdrey, not D. B. Close, was named as captain.

In his bitter disappointment Close played a notable innings of 98 to prevent a Yorkshire collapse at Middlesbrough where Warwickshire were eventually routed, and though he ended his championship batting with a 0 at Harrogate he took the last wicket of a match in which Gloucestershire were defeated by an innings in two days after they had sent Yorkshire in first. The decision was misguided. Before the pitch dried to awkwardness Boycott and Sharpe had raised a partnership of 127 and on the second day the ball turned so readily and incalculably that Illingworth helped himself to 14 wickets, the seven in Gloucestershire's follow-on costing him six runs in 13 overs.

For Close the end of the season was a mental and physical mercy. He was a discarded England captain and a reprimanded captain of the champion county. He was an injured cricketer, struck a glancing blow on the temple when fielding at silly point. He did not play in the final match of the Scarborough Festival. He needed rest and he needed privacy.

32

Vacancies arising

The Yorkshire team photograph for 1968 expresses smiling satisfaction over a championship retained through a third successive season. All the 12 players in the picture are entitled to wear the first-team cap. Close is in the captain's place with Trueman, Illingworth, Binks and Taylor, the seniors, seated beside him; behind stand Boycott, Hampshire, Nicholson, Hutton, Wilson, Padgett and Sharpe, arranged more for pictorial balance than in any order of merit or usefulness.

Order of merit, apart from being invidious, would have been difficult to compose. No individual enjoyed an outstandingly successful season, one was excluded permanently from the regular side; the overall Yorkshire were good enough to win the county championship in a year of undistinguished county cricket. Their advantage over challengers lay mainly in their well-organised and competent fielding.

Boycott showed the best of form at the beginning of the season and in the Scarborough Festival, but he was lost to Yorkshire and to England after the Edgbaston Test in mid-July, when he suffered a back injury, and at one time or another Close, Trueman and Nicholson were compelled to report themselves unfit. Their absences were not disastrously disruptive because they served as a political convenience in helping to solve problems of selection. Close and Trueman were temporarily at odds when Trueman was omitted from the side on Close's judgement of form, but Trueman's spirits recovered when he was required to act as captain. In the absence of Trueman or Nicholson room could be found for Hutton.

Yorkshire's most profitable match of the season, in terms of championship points which included a theoretically unlimited bonus, was at Headingley where they defeated Lancashire by an innings and 56 runs, but the Sheffield fixtures contained the most absorbing cricket.

There Leicestershire were firmly defeated through accumuating advantage in each day and each phase of the match. There Glamorgan won, essentially because Yorkshire balanced the probability of defeat against the possibility of winning through third-day declarations after second-day rain. There a breathtaking struggle with Worcestershire was not fairly measured by the four-wicket margin of Yorkshire victory, for the game was delicately balanced to the last overs.

It was played on a drying pitch that encouraged spin bowling and demanded skilful and resolute batting. After a long-delayed start Worcestershire were put out for 99, Illingworth taking six wickets. Yorkshire were 20 runs behind on first innings and Gifford's bowling figures were eight for 28. In Worcestershire's second innings of 105 D'Oliveira scored 51. On the third morning Yorkshire needed 59 runs from the seven wickets in hand and forced the issue with determined on-side hitting by Hampshire.

The outstanding Sheffield satisfaction of the year, though, was outside championship cricket. On July 1, 2, 3 Yorkshire played the Australians and defeated them by an innings and 69 runs. Throughout the match the county played the dominating cricket. They began with a first-wicket partnership of 105 by Boycott and Sharpe when more experienced swing bowling would have anticipated reward in the heavy morning atmosphere. Persistent batting raised a total of 355 for nine wickets before Truman made a declaration timed to be as inconvenient as possible for Australia, who lost two wickets in half an hour before lunch.

The Australians never recovered from disadvantage. They batted uncomfortably through an afternoon of dim light and suspicion of spin bowling. Trueman, revelling in authority, led his side to conviction of fortune's favours by holding three slip catches, running out Chappell and choosing himself as bowler to end the innings. In the late evening follow-on, Lawry, the foundation of Australian batting obstruction, was yorked for 0.

On the last day the Australians reached 105 for three by

lunchtime, but Yorkshire's control and Trueman's personal incidence were not to be denied. In Trueman's first over of the afternoon Walters, Australia's highest scorer with 62, was caught in the gully. Deteriorating light demanded a tactful withdrawal of the faster bowling but the batsmen found little assurance against Illingworth and Wilson and when the heavier clouds passed to permit Trueman to put himself on again he promptly took the seventh wicket. Yorkshire surged confidently to their victory.

The appointed captain, Close, also contrived memorable occasions for himself during 1968. At Old Trafford he played an innings of character to raise controversy by saving Yorkshire from defeat in a match they were not strong enough to win. The drama of the weekend was contained in the first and last days. Lancashire concluded Saturday's play by taking eight Yorkshire wickets for 34 runs after yielding up their own innings for a total of 162. In the final demand Yorkshire needed 253 with five hours left for play.

Close stayed through all those hours to be 77 not out when stumps were drawn with Yorkshire at 189 for five. Close went in first presumably because he considered himself the most likely batsman to control a situation that had to be assessed and reassessed in relation to the course of events and opportunities arising.

In the beginning the strategy was uncomplicated. Lancashire were bowling to win and Yorkshire were batting to win, though in the mind of both sides lay resolution not to be defeated. Lancashire bowled steadily enough to keep their own prospects bright and to thrust the responsibility for dangerous adventure on Yorkshire. The third wicket fell at 69 after an hour and 40 minutes.

In the afternoon batsmen made their challenge for advantage and victory in a fourth-wicket stand of 79 but bowlers resisted manifest attempts to accelerate the scoring rate. They ended Illingworth's effort by inducing mis-hit to deep mid-off and they frustrated Wilson without dismissing him.

The county rules of the year stipulated 20 overs if necessary from the beginning of the last hour and in this period Yorkshire needed 80 runs, Lancashire five wickets. Yorkshire abandoned hope of the runs and scored 16; Lancashire eventually abandoned hope of the wickets, having taken none. Close would not have headed a popularity poll taken among the Old Trafford spectators.

At Hull, in Yorkshire's last championship match, Close was fortune's instrument in a dramatic victory that virtually ended the challenge of competing counties. Yorkshire had more runs in hand than they were likely to concede when Surrey began the fourth innings, but for the championship points desired Yorkshire's bowlers had to complete a task in approximately four hours on a pitch as accommodating to batting as to bowling.

Only when Surrey fell into a disastrous half-hour immediately after lunch were Yorkshire entirely at ease, but complacency faded as the left-handed Younis Ahmed and Pocock constructed a seventh-wicket partnership of notable assurance. Younis placed the ball comfortably between the on-side fieldsmen; Pocock drove Illingworth disparagingly for six.

Bowlers were waiting for a wicket rather than expecting one at any moment when Younis sought a short single beyond Pocock's capacity and Yorkshire had nearly two hours in which to take three wickets. When all but five minutes of the two hours had gone Yorkshire still wanted three wickets. Younis, batting handsomely by standard of both achievement and appearance, had scored 75. Long, concentrating on defence, had reached 22.

Wilson, who had shared most of the afternoon's bowling burden with Illingworth, was brought on again for the penultimate over. He offered half-volley on or near the leg stump and Younis pulled the ball heartily with the middle of the bat. Close at short square leg had no time for either catch or evasion and the ball rebounded from his forearm into the hands of the wicketkeeper.

In the same over Jackman was lbw and in the next Long was caught at the wicket. Yorkshire brushed stardust from the corks before they opened their celebratory champagne.

This match represented a last county appearance for K.

Taylor and 1968 also ended the Yorkshire careers of Trueman and Illingworth. All three made their own decisions.

Taylor, his benefit season completed, decided to emigrate to South Africa. He left no definable gap in the Yorkshire cricket team because he had held a general rather than a precise place. He had served as an opening batsman and as a middle-order batsman, a bowler of 'little seamers', as he described his own medium-pace swing, and a fieldsman of uncommon mobility, particularly in the covers.

His talent in sport was difficult to assess. In his best innings he played with such fluency and authority that he looked to be of the highest quality, but he seemed to approach his cricket with reservation, as though his essential interest were elsewhere. He could never be accused of being blatantly irresponsible but he gave an impression of using professional sport to serve a purpose of the moment, not as a devotion.

When he was out of form he was bewilderingly vulnerable. Without apparent breakdown of the mechanics he would be clean bowled or leg-before simply through playing where the ball was not, yet in periods of failure and success he maintained the same air of self-sufficiency that made him a player in a team more than a member of a community.

Illingworth and Trueman also left Yorkshire in 1968, Trueman by formal retirement from first-class cricket, Illingworth to seek more profitable terms elsewhere. In pay negotiations for future years Yorkshire were not prepared to abandon their practice of annual engagement for players. Illingworth, at the age of 36, wanted a three- or four-year engagement for himself and made formal request for release from Yorkshire service. Yorkshire complied without hesitation and raised no obstacle to Illingworth's negotiations with other counties or to his registradition for Leicestershire in 1969.

Illingworth found early recognition for his all-round talents and played for Yorkshire in 17 seasons, scoring some 15,000 runs and taking 1,400 wickets. His was a gradual rise to county distinction and Test-match status and his season's figures were never startling in themselves, but they measured an increasing value to Yorkshire sides. In his maturity Illingworth was

Yorkshire's most dependable bowler and most adaptable middle-order batsman. His cricketing views and his cricketing performances were invariably logical. He rarely missed opportunities for profitable off-spin, though he was equally rarely subject to dramatic inspiration. His range was narrow but it was at a high level of technical accomplishment and with excellent fielding added to his bowling and batting Illingworth's cricket was never a handicap to Yorkshire or to England.

Trueman announced his retirement in the November of 1968 proposing for himself a career in different forms of public entertainment. Whatever else he may do or become he will be remembered as a cricketer who took more than 2,300 wickets, mainly by fast bowling that was as thrilling to behold as it was demanding to meet.

Trueman's cricket drew response from both student and the simpler spectator. His bowling gave satisfaction through its vigour and by its sophistication. Greatness was in him and it was not obscured. He left a clear picture in the mind.

Through all his 20 years in the first-class field Trueman was a dramatic cricketer. He raised play to climax and dropped it to anticlimax. He created response and he responded to the response of his own creation. He knew both hero-worship and public condemnation and his resilience of spirit was as marked as the physical power that gave him such remarkable freedom from injury over the years.

Without the exuberance that led him into triumph, disaster and controversy he would not have been the bowler he was, but when the trappings of idiosyncrasy have been discarded by history his ability in fast bowling will be seen on a basis of classical action and trade learned from apprenticeship to master's mark. Trueman proclaimed himself, loudly and at length, a Yorkshireman and Yorkshire cricket need evince no shame in acknowledging his place in the game. In an XI representing all the county history he would be selected.

33

Seen in context

An individual cricketer or a team cannot be assessed in fixed terms of ability, even by comparison of achievements. True greatness may be recognisable but it must remain beyond precise definition and evaluation of attainments involves consideration of circumstances. Theoretically, the greatest players should be the latest players because they have benefit of the experiments and experiences of their predecessors, but in practice each generation tends to restrict itself to the demands of its own time. There is no knowing if Grace and Hutton could have exchanged birth dates and still reached comparable distinction; only opinion rates the team of one period stronger or weaker than the team of another period. The yardstick of judgement must be relation of the possible to the actual. What has been done can be done and inability to do it again may be rated a fall from perfection though not necessarily a failure in current context.

This assumption, expressed in more personal terms, was a burden of complaint from J. V. Wilson when he was Yorkshire's captain. 'We know,' he said, in effect, 'we are not as good as other Yorkshire teams. Judge us by what we do, not by what we should be doing.'

The Yorkshire teams led by J. V. Wilson and Close won championships in a period when county cricket was overshadowed by Test matches and novel forms of cricket demanding attention from county players. The county, as a cricketing unit, had lost some of its significance and the publicity that creates as well as reflects public interest tended to concentrate on other topics.

In the 1950s counties were measured essentially against

Surrey, who won the championship for seven seasons in succession, mainly in conditions peculiarly suited to the bowling of Lock and Laker. Yorkshire were the principal challengers of the period, but they rarely showed themselves likely to establish superiority.

Between the two wars the championship contained a wide discrepancy between the stronger and the weaker teams. Year after year the same teams were at or near the top of the table and the same teams struggled at or near the bottom. Half the fixture list offered predictable results but in the other half meetings of the mighty represented notable occasion. Yorkshire, Lancashire, Middlesex and Nottinghamshire were invariably in dispute for the year's honours and Derbyshire, in 1936, were the only county outside these four to win the championship from 1919 to 1939. Surrey were attractive in batting, Sussex were appreciated for the bowling of Tate, the batting of Duleepsinhji and their tradition of fine fielding. There were foothills to the championship but the winners were required to serve as Everest in the Himalayas.

Kent, whose cricket was reputable from earliest times because the estates of the county served as a cradle for the game, were among the powerful sides of the Edwardian era when cricket touched its peak of social consequence, with amateur approach exerting influence on the development of professional play. The strong sides, the metropolitan counties, Yorkshire, Lancashire and Nottinghamshire, overwhelmed the weak and monopolised the honours, Warwickshire's success of 1911 emphasising the general by interpolation of the particular. Yorkshire's achievements of 1900-1-2 were a creation. No county had previously shown such dominance in priority among equals.

The championship won no official recognition before 1890, though it may be said to have had a regularised existence from 1873 when playing qualifications in a simple form were agreed. Through the cricket Press the championship certainly claimed a public acknowledgement long before it was given a constitution and of the eight or nine counties generally accepted as first-class Gloucestershire and Nottinghamshire set the standards through the 1870s and 1880s.

Standing against the background of cricket Yorkshire can see themselves important among the undistinguished and preeminent among the eminent. There is no means of calculating when they were or will be at their best.